Wrightslaw

Special Education
Legal Developments and Cases
2017

Peter W. D. Wright, Esq.
Pamela Darr Wright, MA, MSW

Harbor House Law Press, Inc.
Hartfield, Virginia 23071

Wrightslaw: Special Education Legal Developments and Cases 2017

By Peter W. D. Wright and Pamela Darr Wright

Library of Congress Cataloging-in-Publication Data

Wright, Peter W. D. and Pamela Darr Wright

Wrightslaw: Special Education Legal Developments and Cases 2017

p. cm.

ISBN 13: 978-1-892320-43-8

ISBN 10: 1-892320-43-6

1. Law — Special Education — United States.   2. Children with disabilities — Education — United States.
3. Special education — Parent Participation — United States. I. Title.

10 9 8 7 6 5 4 3 2 1

Printing History

Harbor House Law Press, Inc. issues new editions to keep our publications current. New editions include major revisions of text and/or changes. New printings include minor changes and corrections.

First Edition   July 2018

Disclaimer

The purpose of this book is to educate and inform. Although efforts have been made to ensure that the publication is accurate, there may be mistakes, typographical and in content. If you are dissatisfied with the book, please return it to the publisher for a full refund.

When You Use a Self-Help Law Book

Law is always changing. The information contained in this book may or may not reflect current legal developments. For legal advice, you should consult with an attorney.

Bulk Purchases

Harbor House Law Press books are available at a discount for bulk purchases, academic sales or textbook adoptions. For information, contact Harbor House Law Press, P. O. Box 480, Hartfield, VA 23071. Please provide the title of the book, ISBN number, quantity, how the book will be used, and date needed.

Toll Free Phone Orders: (877) LAW IDEA or (877) 529-4332.

Toll Free Fax Orders: (800) 863-5348

Dedication

We dedicate this book to Kayla Bower and Patricia Roberts, our co-founders in developing the Institute of Special Education Advocacy (ISEA) at William & Mary Law School.

As co-founders of ISEA, we believe the Institute represents what began three centuries ago at William & Mary. In 1779, Thomas Jefferson founded William & Mary Law School to train leaders for the new nation. Now in its third century, America's oldest law school continues its historic mission of training tireless advocates who are prepared to lead and to serve in their communities.

Kayla Bower, former Director of the Oklahoma Disability Law Center, designed and implemented a curriculum to train special education advocates. She tailored universally recognized ethical standards to special education advocacy. Kayla challenged graduates of ISEA to make ethical decisions in their advocacy.

We are deeply grateful to our friend, Professor Patricia E. Roberts, Vice Dean of the William & Mary Law School, Clinical Professor of Law, and co-director of the Lewis B. Puller Jr. Veterans Benefits Clinic, for her outstanding leadership in developing the Institute of Special Education Advocacy and the PELE Special Education Clinic. Patty brought intelligence, organization, and commitment to these endeavors, ensuring their success.

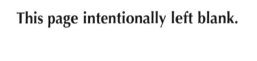
This page intentionally left blank.

Table of Contents

How to Purchase the E-book PDF

This publication is available as a searchable e-book (PDF) from Wrightslaw (immediate download) at http://www.wrightslaw.com/store/2017law.html

When you see a case in the Table of Decisions, you can click on a link that will take you to the comprehensive Summaries of Decisions. All hyperlinks in the PDF download are active.

This page intentionally left blank.

Chapter 1. Legal Concepts and Education Laws

Overview

Studying and reading federal court opinions at the U.S. District Court or U.S. Court of Appeals levels can be a slow frustrating process. However, to truly understand the legal significance of a case, it is necessary for you to develop a clear handle on the issues of a case and the outcome.

When you read articles about a case, you are reading the authors' words which often reflect their personal biases. These articles may not even quote the reasoning for the decision. As a result, your understanding of the case will be limited. To understand a decision, you must take the hard road. Read the original opinion issued by the court several times. Do not rely upon the opinions of others.

How This Book is Organized

Chapter One includes an overview of the legal terms, concepts, and statutes related to special education law.

Chapter Two describes the legal process–the steps in resolving a special education dispute – from the initial request for a due process hearing through appeals to the U.S. District Court, the U.S. Court of Appeals, and the U.S. Supreme Court.

Chapter Three is about how to find cases using "Google Scholar."

Chapter Four includes a Table of Special Education Cases with date, court, issues, and outcome. The cases are linked to a comprehensive discussion of the case, including prevailing party and outcome.

Chapter Five includes discussions of the Court of Appeals cases. We keep interpretations of the rulings to a minimum and instead provide text from the decisions.

Chapter Six includes two special education cases decided by the U.S. Supreme Court in 2017: *Fry v. Napoleon Comm. Sch. Dist.* and *Endrew F. v. Douglas Co. Sch. District*. This chapter includes the full text of both decisions, the Syllabi prepared by the Reporter of Decisions for the convenience of the reader and the Transcripts of Remarks by the Justices when they announced the decisions.

If you have the adobe.pdf version of this book, you will see active hyperlinks. The hyperlinks allow you to jump from a case listed in Chapter Four (Table of Cases) to the discussion of that case in Chapter Five. Other hyperlinks are located throughout this book.

You can also use the "Search" and "Find" features. "Search" is a fast, easy way to find the information you need.

In this chapter, you will learn about the four types of law: federal and state constitutions, statutes, regulations, and case law.

Types of Law

There are four types of law: federal and state constitutions, statutes, regulations, and case law.

Case law refers to judicial interpretations of statutes and regulations that cause law to evolve and change. The essence of this book is focused on case law generated by the U.S. Court of Appeals, the Courts that are one step below the U.S. Supreme Court. In 2017, the U.S. Supreme Court issued two, unanimous, pro-child decisions. The full text, syllabus, and the transcript of Justice Kagan's and Chief Justice Roberts' remarks when they announced their respective decisions are included at the end of this book.

Constitutional Law

The United States Constitution outlines the structure of the federal government. All laws passed must agree with the principles and rights set forth in the Constitution.

The first ten amendments to the Constitution are the Bill of Rights. The Bill of Rights is the source of the most fundamental rights – freedom of speech and religion, protection against unreasonable searches and seizures, and protection from cruel and unusual punishment.

The Fourteenth Amendment, added later, is titled "Civil Rights," but is better known as the "Equal Protection Clause." These Amendments were added to the Constitution to protect citizens against interference from the federal government.

States must ensure that their statutes and regulations are consistent with the United States Code (U.S.C.) and the Code of Federal Regulations (C.F.R.). While state statutes and regulations may provide more rights than federal laws, they cannot provide fewer rights than guaranteed by federal law. If a state law or regulation is in direct conflict with a federal law, federal law controls pursuant to the "Supremacy Clause" of the U.S. Constitution.

Federal Statutes

Statutes are laws passed by federal, state, and local legislatures. In special education jargon, a reference to the "Code," is typically a reference to the statute known as the Individuals with Disabilities Education Act which is located in the United States Code in Title 20 of Section 1400 and cited as 20 U.S.C. §1400. The last revision was in 2004 so it is often referred to as "IDEA 2004" to differentiate it from the former version issued in 1997, known as "ISEA 97."

In addition to IDEA, other federal statutes affecting the education of children with disabilities, are:

- Section 504 of the Rehabilitation Act which begins at 29 U.S.C. § 794 *et seq.*

- The Americans with Disabilities Act Amendments Act of 2008, known as ADA AA, which begins at 42 USCA § 12101, *et seq.*

- Every Student Succeeds Act of 2015 (ESSA), successor to the No Child Left Behind Act of 2001 and a reauthorization of the Elementary and Secondary Education Act of 1965 (ESEA), which begins at 20 U.S.C. § 6301, *et seq.*

- Family Educational and Rights and Privacy Act, known as FERPA, which begins at 20 U.S.C. § 1232, *et seq.*

- McKinney-Vento Homeless Assistance Act which begins at 42 U.S.C. § 11431, *et seq.*

Federal Regulations

After Congress reauthorized the Individuals with Disabilities Education Act in 2004, the U.S. Department of Education (ED) developed proposed special education regulations. The ED published the proposed regulations in the Federal Register (F.R.) and solicited comments from citizens and stakeholders.

On August 14, 2006, the final IDEA 2004 Regulations and an "Analysis of Comments and Changes" known as the "Commentary" was published in the Federal Register. The "Commentary" includes many questions and answers provided by the U.S. Department of Education about those regulations. The full text and specific portions of the Commentary, including the Commentary about IEPs, is located in the Law Library / "IDEA 2004" page on the Wrightslaw.com site.

The IDEA 2004 regulations are published in Volume 34, Part 300 of the Code of Federal Regulations. The legal citation for the regulations is 34 C.F.R. Part 300.

Regulations must be consistent with the law. Regulations may provide more details and specifics than the statute. Regulations are considered to have the "force of law."

Wrightslaw: Special Education Law, **2ⁿᵈ Ed.,** hereinafter referred to as *Wrightslaw*, contains the full text of the statute, i.e., IDEA 2004, and implementing federal regulations. It also includes portions of the other federal statutes listed above.

State Law and Regulations

State constitutions establish the structure of state government. To receive federal special education funds, states must develop special education statutes and regulations that are consistent with the United States Code (U.S.C.) and the Code of Federal Regulations (C.F.R.).

State statutes and regulations may provide more rights than federal law but may not take away rights provided by federal law. When trying to find the answer to a legal question, it is important to begin with the Code, i.e., IDEA 2004, then look at the corresponding federal regulation.

After you understand the federal law and regulation, read your state special education statute and regulation. In many cases, you will find that your state laws and regulations are a verbatim "copy and paste" of the federal law, but not always. Note any differences between federal and state law. Most states have very few special education statutes, with the bulk of state law contained in the state regulations.

If a state law or regulation is in direct conflict with a federal law, federal law controls, pursuant to the "Supremacy Clause" of the U.S. Constitution.

Evolving Case Law & Legal Interpretations

Case Law

As you read the decisions in this book, you will see inconsistencies from one court to another. You will also see how an issue, like "Exhaustion," is evolving from decisions issued just a few years ago.

In 2017, the U.S. Supreme Court issued decisions in two special education cases: *Fry v. Napoleon Comm. Sch. Dist.* and *Endrew F. v. Douglas Co. Sch. District.* Both decisions were unanimous.

Legal Interpretations

Law is subject to different interpretations. If you read an article about a special education decision, the interpretations and conclusions in that article will reflect the opinions and biases of the author. If you read the case on your own, your interpretations and conclusions of the case may be quite different. This is why it is so important for you to read cases, statutes, and regulations yourself, instead of relying on the opinions of others.

When a case has compelling facts, the judge(s) may write a decision that is contrary to the current case law in that Circuit. To support this decision, the judge may find and use unique facts within the case or a loophole in the law to create an "exception to the general rule." Decisions that are "exceptions to the general rule" cause the body of law to change and grow.

When Congress wants to pass a law but cannot agree on the precise wording of the proposed statute, members often compromise by using vague language in the bill. Vague words and phrases in statutes are confusing but are normal in all laws.

Assume you are researching a legal issue and find a U.S. Court of Appeals decision directly related to your issue. You will want to read the earlier U.S. District Court decision that triggered the appeal. When you read the earlier decision, you will have a clearer sense about other, unwritten factors may have affected the decision. You will also see how the law on this issue is evolving in your Circuit. As you read decisions from other Circuits, you will be in a stronger position to understand the evolution of that legal issue.

When one court takes a position that the law is clear, another court may interpret the law differently and arrive at a different opinion. This is the nature of law.

Legal Citations - U.S.C. / F.3d

References to law are called legal citations. Legal citations are standardized formats that describe where you will find a statute, regulation or case. When you see a legal citation such as 20 U.S.C. § 1400 *et seq.*, the term "*et seq.*" means beginning in Volume 20 of the United States Code at Section 1400 and continuing thereafter.

In the United States Code, the "Findings and Purposes" of the Individuals with Disabilities Education Act (IDEA) are in Section 1400 of Title 20. The legal citation for Findings and Purposes is 20 U.S.C. § 1400. You may refer to Findings and Purposes as "20 U.S.C. § 1400" or "Section 1400."

Legal decisions issued by Courts of Appeal are published in the **Federal Reporter, Third Edition.** These decisions are cited by volume number, F.3d, followed by page number, with the Circuit and year in parentheses.

Decisions in the first edition of the **Federal Reporter**, published between 1825 and 1925, are cited as F.1d. Decisions issued between 1925 and 1993 were published in F.2d. In 1993, the first edition of F.3d was published. The third edition of the **Federal Reporter** for Courts of Appeal decisions is now in the 880's. After publication of 999 F.3, legal citations will change to the Fourth Edition.

Some cases in this book were published in the *Federal Reporter, Third Edition* but there is no "F.3d" legal citation for most cases. Later, a few cases in this book that do not currently have a F.3d citation may be published in F.3d. When a Court of Appeals believes that a decision is not noteworthy or does not create new law, that case is not recommended for publication in the *Federal Reporter*, i.e., F.3d.

This book contains nearly every decision related to a special education legal issue issued by U.S. Court of Appeals in 2017. A few decisions were not included because they were quite short, usually one-page, and did not include information of substance about the facts and legal issues in the case.

If you use Google Scholar and read the full text of some of these cases, you may notice a statement at the beginning such as "Not Precedential" or "Do Not Publish" or "Not for Publication." This does not mean you cannot publish the decision or that you cannot rely on the decision as law.

Unless a decision includes other restrictions, "Do Not Publish" usually means that, in the opinion of the judges on that panel, the decision is not noteworthy, does not create new legal precedent, and should not be published in the *Federal Reporter*.

The notation "Do Not Publish" is addressed in Rule 32.1, "Citing Judicial Dispositions," in the Federal Rules of Appellate Procedure (FRAP).

All cases in this book are available from Google Scholar, a publicly accessible electronic database. They can be shared and disseminated. You will learn how to find the full text of the cases on Google Scholar in Chapter 3.

This page intentionally left blank for your notes.

Chapter 2.
The Legal Process

Most disputes between parents of children with special education needs and school districts arise from issues related to eligibility for services, adequacy and implementation of the IEP, tuition reimbursement for private school tuition, and allegations related to bullying and abuse.

There are several methods to resolve disputes between parents and school districts. One, involving litigation, requires the filing of a request for a due process hearing against the school district. Other ways to resolve disputes include mediation, filing an administrative complaint with the state department of education or a federal agency such as the Office of Civil Rights or Department of Justice.

Special Education Due Process Hearings

If you may be involved as a party in a special education due process hearing, you must become familiar with Section 1415 (20 U.S.C. §1415) of the Individuals with Disabilities Education Act (IDEA 2004) and with the federal special education regulations governing due process hearings contained in the Code of Federal Regulations. This portion of the federal regulations is titled "Due Process Procedures for Parents and Children" (34 C.F.R. §300.500).

Wrightslaw: Special Education Law, 2nd Ed., referred to as *Wrightslaw*, contains the complete statute, i.e., IDEA 2004 and all federal regulations. The statute with explanations is at 20 U.S.C. §1415 and begins on page 107. The regulations governing due process regulations is at 34 C.F.R. §300.500, beginning on page 251.

In addition to becoming familiar with the federal statute (United States Code – 20 U.S.C. §1400 *et seq.*) and federal special education regulations (34 C.F.R. Part 300), you must also be familiar with your state's statutes and regulations about due process hearings. You can locate your state's laws about special education by "Googling" the phrase "Yourstatename special education laws rules regulations." In most cases, the first suggested link will take you to your state's page that provides the complete regulations.

Your state's statute and regulations will also provide the title of the individual who conducts hearings, listens to the evidence and issues a ruling. In most states, this individual is called a Hearing Officer (HO), Independent Hearing Officer, Impartial Hearing Officer, or Initial Hearing Officer (IHO). In a few states, this individual is known as an Administrative Law Judge (ALJ).

Your state statute and regulations will also describe the process to initiate a due process hearing. This may require filing a complaint with your State Department of Education (DOE) or, in some instances, with the State's Office of Administrative Hearings (OAH).

Knowing where and how to file the Due Process Complaint Notice, other procedural matters, appellate procedures, and timelines, vary from state to state and a misstep can be fatal to a case.

After the Complainant, who is most often the parent, files the Due Process Complaint Notice (20 U.S.C. §1415(c)(2)(A) - *Wrightslaw*, page 109), the other party, i.e., often known as the Respondent, pursuant to subsection (B) must file "a response that specifically addresses the issues raised in the complaint."

The special education due process hearing is essentially a trial and often includes lay witnesses, expert witnesses, exhibits, testimony, and briefs filed by the parties.

After the final decision is issued, the losing party has the right to appeal. In most states, the losing party at a due process hearing appeals directly to either state or federal court. Those states are known as "Single-Tier States." The federal court is known as the U.S. District Court.

In some states, including Kansas, New York, North Carolina, Ohio, Oklahoma, and South Carolina, an appeal is made to the State Department of Education for appointment of a Reviewing Officer (RO), State Review Officer (SRO) or a Review Panel. States with this second appellate level are known as "Two-Tier States." The losing party at the review level can then appeal directly to either state or federal court.

Appeal to the U.S. District Court

Most special education due process appeals to Court are filed in a U.S. District Court, not in a state court.

If a special education case appeal is filed in state court and it has a "Federal Question" as a possible issue, as a matter of right, the other party can "remove" the case directly to federal court, i.e. the U.S. District Court. Most special education cases have a "Federal Question" as the issue, such as whether the IEP, as defined in federal law, i.e., 20 U.S.C. §1414(d) (*Wrightslaw*, page 99) provides the child with a "free, appropriate public education" (FAPE).

Typically, the complete lower level record, including trial transcripts, trial exhibits, decisions, and sometimes the briefs filed at the lower level, is filed with the U.S. District Court. The party taking the case up on appeal to the U.S. District Court initiates this process by filing a "Complaint" which provides the history of the case, factual and legal, and the legal basis for the desired relief. The other party files a responsive pleading, which might be an "Answer" or a "Motion to Dismiss" or other pleading. These procedures are described in the Federal Rules of Civil Procedure (Fed. R. Civ. P.) and by that particular U.S. District Court's Local Rules of Practice.

At that federal court level, dependent upon local rules of practice and caseload, the U.S. District Court Judge may assign the case to a federal Magistrate Judge who essentially acts in the capacity of the U.S. District Court Judge. The Judge, whether a Magistrate Judge or full U.S. District Court Judge rarely receives new evidence about the case. Instead the Judge generally reviews the lower level decision(s), the exhibits, the trial transcripts and sometimes the pleadings previously filed in the case.

Motions for Judgment on the Administrative Record or Motions for Summary Judgment are filed by one or both parties and the decision issued by that federal judge will usually explain the legal process, discuss the Motions filed by the parties, the standards for reviewing the Motions, explain each party's argument, and the legal and factual background of the case.

After the U.S. District Court has issued its final ruling, the losing party can appeal the case to the U.S. Court of Appeals for that Circuit.

Appeal to the U.S. Courts of Appeals

The U.S. Court of Appeals includes thirteen Circuits around the country. Each Circuit has a panel of Judges. Cases before the U.S. Court of Appeals are heard by three Circuit Court Judges. In some instances, one of the sitting Judges might be a U.S. District Court or even a retired U.S. Supreme Court Justice.

Table 1. U.S. Courts of Appeals

Circuit	States	Circuit	States
1st	MA, ME, NH, RI, PR	7th	IL, IN, WI
2nd	CT, NY, VT	8th	AR, IA, MN, MO, ND, NE, SD
3rd	DE, NJ, PA, USVI	9th	AK, AZ, CA, GU, HI, ID, MT, NV, OR, WA
4th	MD, NC, SC, VA, WV	10th	CO, KS, NM, OK, UT, WY
5th	LA, MS, TX	11th	AL, FL, GA
6th	KY, MI, OH TN	DC	Washington, D.C.

One Court of Appeals is not included in Table 1. The Thirteenth Circuit, known as the "Federal Circuit," primarily hears patent case appeals and is not geographically based.

In this Table of Cases, you see that any case from a U.S. District Court from the state of New York must be filed in the U.S. Court of Appeals for the Second Circuit. Any case from a U.S. District Court in California must be filed in the U.S. Court of Appeals for the Ninth Circuit.

The Index at the end of this book includes a list of Court of Appeals cases by Circuit with sub-listings of the District Court of origin.

In 2017, Courts of Appeals issued rulings in eleven cases from New York (Second Circuit), five from California (Ninth Circuit), four from Pennsylvania (Third Circuit) and Texas (Fifth Circuit), three from Hawaii (Ninth Circuit), two from Alabama, Maryland, and Minnesota (Eleventh, Fourth, and Eighth respectively), and one from the remaining states. All eleven cases appealed to the Second Circuit were from the state of New York; six cases included the New York City Department of Education as a party.

When you look at the Ninth Circuit, you see that five of the eight cases were from a U.S. District Court in California and three were from the U.S. District Court in Hawaii.

Filing and timeline rules for U.S. Courts of Appeals are provided in the Federal Rules of Appellate Procedure (Fed. R. App. P. // FRAP). Like due process regulations and the Federal Rules of Civil Procedure, one misstep, a failure to file within a specified timeline, or other error is often fatal to a case. When cases are submitted to the Courts of Appeals, no new evidence or testimony is submitted.

After Briefs and sometimes after Oral Argument, the Court of Appeals will issue a final ruling. This ruling may affirm i.e., uphold the ruling of the U.S. District Court, reverse the earlier ruling, or dismiss some claims and reverse others. In some instances, the appellate court will remand all or part of the case back to the U.S. District Court.

After an adverse ruling, the losing party can Petition the Court for a Rehearing or for an *en banc* hearing i.e., before a much larger and often, full panel of the Judges sitting on the Court of Appeals.

After the case has ended at the Court of Appeals level, the losing party can then file a Petition with the U. S. Supreme Court to request a *Writ of Certiorari*.

Appeal to the U.S. Supreme Court (SCOTUS)

The U. S. Supreme Court, often referred to in the legal community and this book as "SCOTUS," only accepts 100-150 of the more than 7,000 cases that it is asked to review each year. Filing a Petition for a *Writ of Certiorari* is a request that SCOTUS hear the case. The Petition generally does not argue the nature of the alleged errors committed by the U.S. Court of Appeals, but instead argues why SCOTUS should agree to hear the case.

"A Petition for a Writ of Certiorari is rarely granted when the asserted error consists of erroneous factual findings or the misapplication of a properly stated rule of law." (Rule 10 of the Rules of the Supreme Court of the United States.)

"The Supreme Court has its own set of rules. According to these rules, four of the nine Justices must vote to accept a case." (Source of preceding quotes – SCOTUS website.)

Like the preceding lower level courts, there are strict rules which are available online.

The best route to SCOTUS acceptance of an appeal from the U.S. Court of Appeals and issuance of a "*Writ of Certiorari*" is that one circuit has issued a ruling that is in direct opposition to the ruling from another circuit.

When a federal judge in your state issues a decision that provides a new definition or legal standard, that decision is binding on the district courts in your state, but it is not binding on U.S. District Court judges in other states.

When a U.S. Court of Appeals issues a decision, that ruling is binding on all federal district courts within that circuit, but it is not binding on other U.S. District Courts and U.S. Court of Appeals in other parts of the country. That decision may, however, be considered "persuasive authority."

Split Between Circuits / U.S. Supreme Court Appeal

It is not unusual for one circuit to issue a ruling that is in direct conflict with another circuit, i.e., a "split between circuits." That's what happened in the author's *Carter* case.

In 1989, the U.S. Court of Appeals for the Second Circuit issued a decision in *Tucker v. Bay Shore Union Free School Dist.*, 873 F.2d 563 (2d.1989). Tucker held that parents could not be reimbursed for private school tuition, even if the public school's IEP was not appropriate, if the private program was not on the state's approved list and the teachers were not certified or licensed by the state.

Later, in *Florence County Sch. Dist. IV v. Carter*, 510 U.S. 7 (1993), the Fourth Circuit held that reimbursement is proper if the private program is appropriate, even if the program is not on the state's approved list and the teachers are not certified by the state.

In a landmark decision, SCOTUS unanimously upheld the Fourth Circuit's decision in *Carter*. This changed the legal landscape for tuition reimbursement cases, often known as *Carter* cases. The decision also opened the door for parents of children with autism who could be reimbursed for the expensive one-on-one ABA "Lovaas" therapy.

When the U. S. Supreme Court issues a ruling, pursuant to the Supremacy Clause of the U. S. Constitution, it becomes the "law of the land" and is binding throughout the country.

In *Special Education Legal Developments and Cases 2015*, we reported on decisions issued by the Sixth Circuit in the *Fry* case and by the Tenth Circuit in *Endrew F.* Both decisions were adverse to the parents.

In the next edition, *Special Education Legal Developments and Cases 2016*, we reviewed the issues in these cases because SCOTUS had granted a *Writ of Certiorari* in both cases.

In Chapter Six of *Special Education Legal Developments and Cases 2017*, you will find the full text of the decisions in *Fry v. Napoleon* and *Endrew F. v. Douglas County* as issued by the U.S. Supreme Court in 2017. We included the transcript of the remarks by Justice Kagan and Chief Justice Roberts when the Justice announced their decision in *Fry v. Napoleon* and *Endrew F. v. Douglas Co.*

This page intentionally left blank for your notes.

This page intentionally left blank for your notes.

Chapter 3. Finding Cases with Google Scholar

In this chapter, you will learn about Google Scholar, the free accessible search engine that indexes the full text of federal and state legal decisions. You will learn how to use Google Scholar to find the full text of decisions in your areas of interest.

Google Scholar allows you to search published opinions of state appellate and supreme courts since 1950, opinions from U.S. District Courts, U.S. Courts of Appeal since 1923, and decisions from the U.S. Supreme Court since 1791.

Google Scholar embeds clickable citation links within cases.

Another portion of Google Scholar searches peer-reviewed papers, theses, books, preprints, abstracts and technical reports from academic publishers, professional societies, preprint repositories and universities, and scholarly articles available on the Internet.

The Mechanics of Using Google Scholar

When you use http://scholar.google.com, you can find any decision listed in the Table of Cases.

Let's find the second case listed in the Table of Cases – *L.K. v. NYC DOE*, a decision issued on January 19, 2017 by the Second Circuit.

Go to: http://scholar.google.com/

Click on "Case law" then "Select courts." When the Courts page opens, go to the right column, "Federal courts," select the "Court of Appeals" for your desired Circuit (2nd Circuit) and click "Done" at the bottom of the page.

A screen will open that instructs you to "Please enter a query in the search box above." You will insert the following, word for word, with the quotation marks" "individuals with disabilities education act"

then add the year, 2017, and an identifiable part of the case name, "L.K."

Your search query should now read: "individuals with disabilities education act" 2017 "L.K." Your screen will look like the image below.

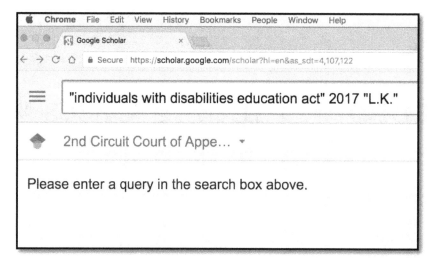

When you hit "Return" on your keyboard, Google Scholar will do a full text search of all cases in their database from the Second Circuit that have those words in your query.

You will see that the *L.K. v. NYC DOE* case was issued on January 19, 2017 by the Second Circuit with a hyperlink to the actual decision. If you click on the **LK** link, you will go directly to the discussion about the case.

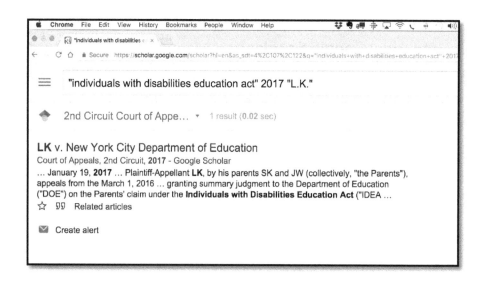

If you edit your search query by deleting "L.K." and changing 2017 to 2018, you will find all cases issued by the Second Circuit in 2018 that contained the exact phrase "individuals with disabilities education act".

If you delete the year, you will find all Second Circuit cases going back over many years. In the right corner of your Google Search screen, you will see the entry "YEAR." When you click on that, you can sort the cases by date. Otherwise you will see listed at the top very old IDEA cases that might reference a page of another case, which happens to be the year you entered.

You can change your search query to look for cases that have other terms — dyslexia, autism, Section 504, restraint, damages, retaliation, "individualized educational program," "IEP," "independent educational evaluation," "IEE," "Americans with Disabilities Act," etc. It is imperative that you use quotation marks, otherwise you will be flooded with cases that are not specific to your search.

When you change the courts, you can broaden your search to find cases around the country. You can even search against the name of an individual, an administrator, an expert witness, a Judge, or a school district.

Troubleshooting

On occasion, you may search for a known case and not be able to find it.

When the authors were creating the database of Court of Appeals cases for *Special Education Legal Developments and Cases 2015,* we knew about a couple of decisions that did not appear when we used the term "Individuals with Disabilities Education Act 2004". We were perplexed. We knew these cases existed but we could not find them.

When we experimented with search terms, we found these cases. In one, the case had a line break inside the word "Education." The word was printed in the full text of the decision as "Educa-tion" so the Google Scholar search engine did not find it.

Two cases from the Ninth Circuit referenced IDEA as the "Individuals with Disabilities Education Improvement Act." When we changed our search term to "Individuals with Disabilities Education Improvement Act," we found the decisions which did not show up in our original search.

Create a Google Scholar Alert

Go back to your original search page. At the bottom of the page, you will see a link to "Create alert." When you create an alert, Google Scholar will send you an email alert whenever a decision is issued in the legal jurisdiction you select.

But don't do this just yet.

Return to the "Select courts" page. Select the Courts of Appeals for all Circuits, all U.S. District Courts in your State, and all your state courts. Change your search query to "Individuals with Disabilities Education Act" 2018 and then do the search again.

You will now see all cases issued to date in 2018. You will also see at the bottom of the page the "Create Alert" icon. You will be asked to enter your email address. After you enter your email address, Google will notify you of all new IDEA decisions from your federal and state courts and from all Courts of Appeal around the country in 2018.

In this chapter, you learned how to use Google Scholar to search for legal decisions. You learned how to expand and narrow your search and how to create a Google Alert.

The next chapter includes the Table of Cases for 2017.

This page intentionally left blank for your notes.

Chapter 4. Table of Decisions

January 1, 2017 through December 31, 2017

This chapter includes a Table of Cases with all significant decisions in special education cases by the U.S. Courts of Appeals from January 1 through December 31, 2017.

The first column in the Table of Cases is the date of the decision. The second column includes the state where the case was litigated and the Judge who authored the Opinion if known. Some cases do not include a Judge's name. These cases are usually identified as "Per Curiam" or "Summary" decisions and are delivered as rulings by the Court acting collectively, not by a judge.

The third column provides the short style or name of the case. Typically, names of the parties are abbreviated. Each case has a bookmark in the style of the case, i.e. *L.K. v. NYC DOE* or *M.C. v Antelope Valley Union High Sch. Dist.* If you have the PDF edition of this book, when you click a bookmark, you will go to a comprehensive discussion of the case in Chapter 5.

The fourth column, Description, describes key legal issues addressed in the ruling, outcome and prevailing party.

If the case was published in the Federal Reporter, Third Edition, (F.3d) at the time this book was published, we provide the legal citation.

Cases in which the Individuals with Disabilities Education Act (IDEA) was not an issue and roughly half a dozen "Summary" decisions by Courts of Appeal that included minimal detail and law are not included in this book.

Table 2. Special Education Decisions in 2017

Date	Circuit State Judge	Short Style F.3d Cite, if any	Description
1/10/2017	2nd NY Wesley	*A.M. v. NYC DOE*	In this tuition reimbursement case, the primary issues were the school district's failure to include ABA methodology in the IEP and failure to properly create a Functional Behavior Assessment (FBA) and formulate a Behavior Intervention Plan (BIP). After the parents lost at all levels, they appealed to the Court of Appeals for the Second Circuit. The Court of Appeals held that the IHO's, SRO's and District Court Judge's reliance on testimony by school psychologist was error "as this resulted a proposed program that was not 'reasonably calculated to enable [E.H.] to receive ... [FAPE].'" Outcome: Reversed and remanded. Parent prevailed.
1/19/2017	2nd NY	*L.K. v. NYC DOE*	This case involved reimbursement for private school tuition and supplemental services pursuant to the *Burlington/Carter* test. The Court upheld denial of private tuition but remanded the case back to the U.S. District Court to determine the amount and extent of reimbursement for supplemental OT services. Outcome: School prevailed on most, but not all issues. Remanded for further proceedings.
1/27/2017	1st ME Stahl	*M. v. Falmouth Sch. Dept.* 847 F.3d 19	In *M. v. Falmouth Sch. Dept*, the parent asserted that the school district failed to provide FAPE because they did not provide her daughter with SPIRE instruction. After the Hearing Officer and U.S. District Court agreed with the parents, the school appealed. The Court of Appeals reversed, explaining that: "O.M.'s IEP did not mandate that Falmouth use SPIRE, meaning the School Department neither breached the IEPs terms nor denied O.M. with a FAPE by foregoing such instruction. Accordingly, we reverse." Outcome: School prevailed.

1/27/2017	2nd NY	*J.D. v. NYC DOE*	In this tuition reimbursement case, the parents argued that their child's 2011 IEP was not appropriate. The IHO and SRO disagreed and denied tuition reimbursement. The Second Circuit held that" "the 2011 IEP … was substantially similar to the 2010 version that the IHO found to be inadequate." "The DOE needed more than conclusory and contradictory testimony from its witnesses." The judgment of the U.S. District Court was reversed and the case remanded. Outcome: Parent prevailed.
1/27/2017	2nd NY	*Luo v. Baldwin Union Free Sch. Dist.*	In this "collateral estoppel" case, the parents represented themselves. Because this case included the same parties and same issue as an earlier case, the Court dismissed under the "doctrine of collateral estoppel." The U.S. District Court excused the school district's late filed answer because of "confusion from Luo's multiple pending actions." Outcome: Case dismissed. School prevailed.
1/30/2017	3rd PA Fisher	*Issa v. Lancaster Sch. Dist.* 847 F.3d 121	In this Pennsylvania case, non-English-speaking school-age refugee children were placed in an "alternative educational program intended to serve 'at-risk Students' … overage for their grade and in danger of not graduating high school before they age out of public-school eligibility at 21." The children sued under the Equal Educational Opportunities Act of 1974 (EEOA), seeking a preliminary injunction ordering placement into "a program designed principally to teach language skills to English language learners, or ELLs." The U.S. District Court ruled in their favor. The school district appealed. The Court of Appeals upheld the ruling in favor of the students. Outcome: Parents prevailed.

2/22/2017	SCOTUS Kagan	**Wrightslaw Summary:** *Fry v. Napoleon Comm. Sch. Dist.* **Syllabus** **Full Text** **Justice Kagan's Transcript**	**Wrightslaw Case of the Year.** *Fry v. Napoleon* is the landmark "Exhaustion of Administrative Remedies" case and one of four Wrightslaw Cases of the Year. In special education disputes, if parents seek an educational remedy, they must exhaust their administrative remedies (request a special education due process hearing) before filing suit in the U.S. District Court. In *Fry*, the parents were not seeking an educational remedy and did not request a due process hearing. The U.S. District Court and U.S. Court of Appeals dismissed their case. The parents appealed to SCOTUS. In a unanimous decision, SCOTUS reversed the 2nd Circuit and held that you must look at the "gravamen," the essence of the case, to see if the remedy the parent sought was or was not educational in nature. **Wrightslaw Note:** Chapter 6 includes the full text of the U.S. Supreme Court's Opinion in *Fry v. Napoleon*, the Syllabus of the case issued by the Reporter of Decisions, and the transcript of Justice Kagan's Announcement of the Opinion in which she summarized the decision in her own words.
3/7/2017 5/11/2017	5th TX Costa	*Reyes v. Manor Indep. Sch. Dist.* 850 F.3d 251	In this Statute of Limitations (SOL) and failure to exhaust administrative remedies case, the parents filed a request for a due process hearing after their son turned 18. The essence of the case related to relief that could have been provided under the IDEA. The Court noted that … "most of the IDEA claims fell outside the one-year window." Outcome: Based on the failure to exhaust and statute of limitations, the dismissal was upheld and school prevailed.
3/7/2017	8th MO Benton	*J.M. v. Francis Howell Sch. Dist.* 850 F.3d 944	The parent of a child with an IEP filed suit against the school district alleging "unlawful use of isolation and physical restraints." The District Court dismissed the case because the parent failed to exhaust her administrative remedies prior to filing suit. While this case was on appeal to Court of Appeals, SCOTUS issued the ruling in *Fry* which clarified the requirement to exhaust should be based on the "gravamen" of the suit.

			Two weeks after *Fry* was issued, decision, the 8th Circuit held that "IDEA's exhaustion requirement remains the general rule, regardless of whether the administrative process offers the particular type of relief that is being sought." Outcome: Dismissal upheld. Parent failed to exhaust, school prevailed.
3/15/2017	9th CA	***S.H. v. Tustin Unif. Sch. Dist.***	In this case, the school district proposed to change a child's educational placement. The parents objected and asserted that the district predetermined the placement, failed to provide proper "Prior Written Notice" and failed to "adequately involve" the parents before arriving at the placement decision. The ALJ, the U.S. District Court, and the Ninth Circuit upheld the district's proposed change of placement as providing FAPE. The Ninth Circuit found that the parents participated in the decision-making process and the school did not predetermine the placement. Outcome: School prevailed.
3/16/2017	7th IL Rovner	***Ostby v. Manhattan Sch. Dist.*** 851 F.3d 677	This case concerns ongoing litigation after a case is "moot". The school wanted to change the child's placement to a different more restrictive school. The parents objected and requested a due process hearing. Pursuant to the "Stay Put" statute, the child remained in the same general education placement with special education support services. This placement continued through the appeal to the U.S. District Court, and their appeal to the Seventh Circuit. The parents lost on the merits at all levels. At the time of Oral Argument before the Seventh Circuit, a new agreed-upon IEP was in place. The placement was in the same general education setting in effect at the beginning of the case. The sole remaining issue was reimbursement for attorneys' fees. The Court provided a comprehensive analysis on the law of "mootness" and dismissed the parent's case as moot. Outcome: School prevailed.

3/21/2017 later SCOTUS vacated, new decision on 2/14/2018	9th CA	*E.F. v. Newport Mesa Unif. Sch. Dist.*	This case is about the "deference" by an appellate judge when a case is appealed from the due process hearing level. Typically, when a case is appealed, the Judge reviews the lower level decision and may review testimony and transcripts but does not hear new evidence.
			The Ninth Circuit did not provide background about the facts in this case. The U.S. District Court Judge noted, "The ALJ found that Plaintiffs had failed to meet their burden of proof … [and] failed to demonstrate that the district's assessments were improper or that the district staff was not properly trained to provide E.F. with instruction or services."
			The Ninth Circuit held that "It was proper for the district court to accord the ALJ's decision substantial deference …"
			Initial Outcome: The Ninth Circuit upheld the OAH and U.S. District Court decisions. School prevailed. In light of their decision in *Endrew F.*, SCOTUS later vacated this decision, new briefs were filed, and the essence of the earlier decision was re-affirmed on February 14, 2018.
			Final Outcome: OAH and the U.S. District Court decision upheld by Ninth Circuit. School prevailed.
3/22/2017	SCOTUS CJ Roberts	**Wrightslaw Summary–** *Endrew F. v. Douglas County Sch. Dist.* **Syllabus** **Full Text** **Chief Justice Roberts' Transcript**	**Wrightslaw Case of the Year** In 1982, SCOTUS defined the term "free appropriate public education" (FAPE) in the *Amy Rowley* case. SCOTUS' decision in *Endrew F.* expanded and partially redefined FAPE.
			Endrew had an IEP from preschool through fourth grade. By fifth grade, his parents believed his academic and functional progress had stalled. The school district proposed an IEP for fifth grade but that IEP resembled IEPs from past years. Endrew's parents removed him from public school and enrolled him in a private school where he made significant progress. The parents sued for tuition reimbursement. They lost at all levels, from Due Process, to District Court and at the Tenth Circuit.
			The HO and Courts stated that the school district's IEP was appropriate because it was calculated to confer an "educational benefit [that is] merely … more than *de minimis* [and had been] reasonably calculated to enable [him] to make some progress."

			The split among circuits revolved around the terms "some educational benefit" versus "meaningful educational benefit."
			The Opinion authored by Chief Justice Roberts reviewed the legal history surrounding FAPE and the 1982 SCOTUS *Rowley* case that defined FAPE:
			"When all is said and done, a student offered an educational program providing 'merely more than *de minimis*' progress from year to year can hardly be said to have been offered an education at all. For children with disabilities, receiving instruction that aims so low would be tantamount to 'sitting idly … awaiting the time when they were old enough to 'drop out.''"
			"The IDEA demands more. It requires an educational program reasonably calculated to enable a child to make progress appropriate in light of the child's circumstances."
			Outcome: The parents prevailed. SCOTUS reversed the earlier decisions; redefined and expanded FAPE, as evidenced by the *Antelope Valley* case, below. The parents prevailed.
3/27/2017 amended 5/30/2017	9th CA Kozinski	*M.C. v Antelope Valley Union High Sch. Dist.* 852 F.3d 840 858 F.3d 1189	**Wrightslaw Case of the Year.** All special education attorneys need to read *MC v. Antelope Valley* because the decision relies on *Endrew F.*, i.e., focus on the child's potential; IEPs are much like contracts; a school district's alteration of an IEP without the parents' knowledge or consent; the threat of sanctions against a school board attorney regarding whether the attorney attempted to mislead the parents and opposing counsel versus "mere bungling" and the school district's failure to file a response to the parents Due Process Complaint Notice. Relying on *Endrew F.*, the Ninth Circuit wrote: "… a school must offer an IEP reasonably calculated to enable a child to make progress appropriate in light of the child's circumstances. In other words, the school must implement an IEP that is reasonably calculated to remediate and, if appropriate, accommodate the child's disabilities so that the child can 'make progress in the general education curriculum,' taking into account the progress of his non-disabled peers, and the child's potential …so the district court can consider plaintiffs' claims in light of this new guidance from the Supreme Court." Outcome: District Court decision reversed, case remanded. The parents prevailed.

3/30/2017	9th WA Christen	*Avila v. Spokane Sch. Dist.* 852 F.3d 936	In this Statute of Limitations (SOL) case, the U.S. District Court barred all claims occurring more than two years before the plaintiffs filed their administrative due process. The Court of Appeals reversed. "Because the district court barred the Avilas' pre-April 2008 claims based on when the district's actions occurred, we remand to the district court to make findings and address the statute of limitations under the standard we adopt here, namely when the Avilas 'knew or should have known about the alleged actions that form the basis of the complaint.'" Outcome: U.S. District Court decision reversed, parents prevailed.
4/13/2017	9th CA	*Irvine Sch. Dist. v. K.G.* 853 F.3d 1087	This attorneys' fee case began in 2007. The Court of Appeals wrote, "We are asked to decide whether the attorney ... is entitled to fees for legal work performed after the student's graduation from public school." After a partial success, the child's attorney became ill, let an attorney fee petition timeline (SOL) pass, the child graduated, and the petition for attorneys' fees was filed with new counsel. The Ninth Circuit allowed the attorney fee issue to be re-opened but limited the award in part because the child had graduated. The Court remanded the case back to the district court to re-evaluate the attorney fee award. Outcome: Partial victory for each party.
4/27/2017	2nd NY	*R.B. v. NYC DOE*	In this tuition reimbursement case, the Hearing Officer (SRO) ruled in favor the parents, finding that the IEPs for the two years prior to the child's removal "were insufficient" and that the parents were entitled to an award of tuition reimbursement. Issues included predetermination of the IEP, inadequate goals, failure to include the child for IEP transition planning, and methodology. NYC appealed this decision to a Review Officer (SRO) who reversed. That reversal was upheld by the U.S. District Court. The parent appealed to the Second Circuit. The Court analyzed each issue and upheld the U.S. District Court's dismissal. Outcome: School prevailed.

4/27/2017	8th AR	*Brittany O. v. Bentonville Sch. Dist.*	The parents' attorney prevailed at a special education due process hearing. The school did not appeal so the parents were entitled to attorneys' fees. The primary issue involved the timeline to file for attorneys' fees. Parents' attorney failed to file for attorneys' fees within the 90-day Arkansas Statute of Limitations (SOL). The U.S. District Court dismissed the case. The Court of Appeals addressed whether the SOL begins after the date of a successful due process decision or after the 90-day SOL timeline for the school to appeal an adverse ruling. The Eighth Circuit reversed the District Court, held that the request was timely filed, affirmed the parents' entitlement to attorneys' fees, Outcome: Parents prevailed.
5/9/2017	2nd NY	*J.C. v. Katonah- Lewisboro Sch. Dist.*	After a due process hearing, the IHO awarded tuition reimbursement. The SRO reversed. The parents appealed to the U.S. District Court which reversed the SRO, explaining that "Courts generally owe deference to the decision of an SRO, but that deference only extends insofar as the SRO decision is well-reasoned and persuasive." The Court of Appeals struck the decision of the SRO and re-instated the decision of the IHO. Outcome: Parents prevailed.
5/23/2017	2nd NY	*D.B. v. Ithaca City Sch. Dist.*	In this tuition reimbursement case, the Second Circuit discussed the three-pronged *Burlington/Carter* test to determine eligibility for reimbursement. The parent attacked the procedural adequacy of the evaluations. The Court held that any procedural testing violations did not deprive child of FAPE. Outcome: Tuition reimbursement denied. School prevailed.
6/2/2017, revised 7/31/2017	5th TX	*D.L. v. Clear Creek Indep. Sch. Dist.*	In this eligibility and "pleadings and practice" case, the school found that a high school student with an IEP was ineligible for special education services. At the end of his senior year, the child was often absent. The parent requested an Independent Educational Evaluation (IEE). The independent evaluator determined that the child should still be eligible for special education services and an IEP. The school disagreed.

			The parent requested a due process hearing. The HO noted that the parent did not allege a "Child Find" violation so did not allow the senior year issues to come into evidence. The HO found that the child did not have a disability and did not need special education services. On appeal, the U.S. District Court and Fifth Circuit upheld this decision. Outcome: School prevailed.
6/14/2017	2nd NY	*C.E. v. Chappaqua Cent. Sch. Dist. + NYDOE*	In this tuition reimbursement case, the IHO, SRO, and U.S. District denied the parents' request for tuition reimbursement. On appeal, the parents claimed that the IHO was and "the IHO's decision should not be afforded deference because he was (1) biased because he had previously been a school superintendent and (2) incompetent because (a) he was not an attorney and (b) he fell asleep during portions of the hearing." The Second Circuit upheld the IHO's decisions because: "The New York regulations 'grandfathered' him" although he was not a lawyer because he was an IHO prior to September 1, 2001. "Further, the IHO also brought decades of experience as a hearing officer to the bench." Outcome: U.S. District Court's ruling upheld; school prevailed.
6/21/2017	9th Hawaii	*I.T. v. Hawaii DOE*	In this appeal of a reduced award of attorneys' fees, the Ninth Circuit discussed a reduction of the requested hourly rate and the impact of limited success. Outcome: the U.S. District Court reduction upheld, state of Hawaii prevailed.
6/23/2017	DC Tatel	*DL v. DCPS* 860 F.3d 713	In this Washington, D.C. "Child Find" class action case, the parents alleged a "pervasive and systemic" breakdown in the district's Child Find program. "These deficiencies, the parents argued, were depriving hundreds of preschoolers of their right to a FAPE." The U.S. District Court "found the district liable for violating its Child Find obligations and failing to ensure a 'smooth and effective transition' for toddlers entering preschool."

			DC Public Schools claimed the case should be dismissed: "As the district sees it, the 'proper role' of IDEA's judicial enforcement provision is individualized rather than systemic relief." The Court of Appeals responded, "So long as the District of Columbia accepts federal funding, it is bound to its pledge to find, evaluate, and serve all children with disabilities. The district court neither erred nor abused its discretion in holding the District to its word." Outcome: Parents prevailed.
6/29/2017 TX Weiner	5th	*C.G. v. Waller Indep. Sch. Dist.*	In this tuition reimbursement case, the Fifth Circuit found that the U.S. District Court's analysis of the public school's IEP was in accord with the SCOTUS ruling in *Endrew F.* and upheld the denial of tuition reimbursement. "Although the district court did not articulate the standard set forth in *Endrew F.* verbatim, its analysis of C.G.'s IEP is fully consistent with that standard and leaves no doubt that the court was convinced that C.G.'s IEP was appropriately ambitious in light of her circumstances." Outcome: School prevailed.
6/29/2017 MN Shepherd	8th	*Special School District 1 v. R.M.M.* 861 F.3d 769	This case addresses whether a child with a disability has IDEA rights while enrolled in a private school under state law, not federal law. The parents requested a special education due process hearing stating that "MPS had denied R.M.M. a free appropriate public education ('FAPE') while R.M.M. was enrolled at her private school." The Court of Appeals noted "Minnesota has long guaranteed special education services for children with disabilities under state law ... A plain reading of Minnesota state law shows that private school students have a right to a FAPE ...Those services cannot be denied to any individual student because he or she attends private school." The Court of Appeals upheld the U.S. District Court ruling that Minnesota law mandates special education services for children enrolled in private schools. Outcome: Parents prevailed.

6/30/2017	9th CA	***R.A. v. West Contra Costa Unif. Sch. Dist.***	Issues in this case included a parent's right to observe a school's evaluation and a one-on-one placement with ABA versus a private school placement. The ALJ and the District Court ruled against the parents, found that the public school IEP was appropriate, the parents had no right to observe the evaluation, the parents proposed placement was not in the least restrictive environment (LRE), and the school did not predetermine the proposed placement. Outcome: School prevailed.
7/14/2017	8th MN Loken	***I.Z.M. v. Rosemount-Apple Valley Eagan Pub. Sch.*** 863 F.3d 966	This post-*Endrew F.* case addressed the appropriateness of an IEP for a child who has severe vision problems. This child's IEP provided that he "will use Braille for all classroom assignments." Dissatisfied with his progress, the parents requested a due process hearing. They argued that state law mandated that their child have "the same level of proficiency expected of the student's peers." In addition to violations of IDEA, Section 504, and ADA, they also argued a violation of the Minnesota Blind Persons' Literacy Rights and Education Act. In ruling for the school, the Eighth Circuit held that "a disabled student's § 504 and ADA claims of unlawful discrimination are not precluded [barred] if they are wholly unrelated to the IEP process." The Court of Appeals did not find violations of Section 504 and ADA and upheld the U.S. District Court's ruling against the parents and child. Outcome: School prevailed.
7/19/2017	3rd NJ Rendell	***C.G.; R.G. v. Winslow Township Bd. Ed.***	This dispute involved recovery of parent's attorney's fees and videotape discovery depositions. The parents' attorney wanted to videotape discovery depositions on his personal laptop computer. The U.S. District Court and the Court of Appeals refused to permit him to tape the depositions and held that the attorney's "well-documented history of egregious conduct in fee requests of grossly overstating his fees shocked the conscience of the District Court." The Court of Appeals upheld the reduction of attorneys' fees from $160,731 to $47,212.50 and upheld the prior rulings on videotaping depositions. Outcome: School prevailed.

7/27/2017	5th TX Southwick	*Dallas Indep. Sch. Dist. v. Woody*	This tuition reimbursement "comparable IEP" case presented a "unique factual situation." The child started high school in a Dallas private school. Later, she moved to Los Angeles, enrolled in a private school, then in a public school where she was found eligible for an IEP. She moved back to Dallas, enrolled in a private school, and the parent sought a private placement under IDEA. Nearly a year after the child returned to Dallas, the school district held an IEP meeting and offered placement in a public school program. The district knew that the child would graduate from the private school the next month. The hearing officer found for the parent (Woody) and awarded her $25,426.93. The district court affirmed but reduced the award to $11,942.50. The school district appealed. Woody did not." Outcome: Parent prevailed. The Court remanded the case back to the U.S. District Court to recalculate the reimbursement award.
8/11/2017	11th AL	*Jefferson County Bd. Ed. v. Brian M, Darcy M*	This is an attorney fee / mootness case in which parents prevailed at a due process hearing. Later, they enrolled their child in a different school. The school district appealed, arguing the case was moot and that the parents were not entitled to reimbursement of their attorney's fees. The Court of Appeals held "In sum, this case is moot, [however] the Parents and R.M. qualify as 'prevailing parties' entitled to reasonable attorney's fees, and the hearing officer's order should not be vacated." Outcome: Parents prevailed.
8/14/2017	4th MD Agee	*M.L. v. Montgomery County Bd. Ed.* *+Supt. Smith* 867 F.3d 487	In this case, parents wanted their school district to include in their child's IEP that their son would be "taught about the Torah, kosher rules, and Orthodox Jewish garments ... [and] 'that he be able to read Hebrew." After the district refused to include religious instruction in the IEP, the parents placed the child into a private school and sought tuition reimbursement. In denying tuition reimbursement, the Fourth Circuit held that "MCPS provided M.L. with equal access to an education, on the same basis as it provides to all other students with disabilities. It does not provide religious and cultural instruction to its students with or without disabilities and has no duty under the IDEA to administer such instruction to M.L." Outcome: School prevailed.

29

8/22/2017	3rd PA Krause	*M.R.; J.R. v. Ridley* *Sch. Dist.* 868 F.3d 218	In this attorneys' fees case, the parents sought tuition reimbursement for a private placement. The Hearing Officer agreed and ordered reimbursement for the private placement. The school district appealed. The U.S. District Court reversed. Parents appealed to the Third Circuit which affirmed the denial of tuition reimbursement. However, from the date of the Hearing Officer's decision, pursuant to the federal special education regulations, that private placement is deemed to be the "current educational placement." Pursuant to the "stay put" statute, the school district was required to pay for the private program until the legal process concluded. The school district refused to reimburse the parents for the private placement. Parents sued for the "stay put" reimbursement and also sued for their attorney's fees for having to pursue that reimbursement. Outcome: Parents prevailed.
8/29/2017	9th HI Fisher	*Rachel H. v. Hawaii* *DOE*	Pursuant to a settlement agreement with DOE, Rachel H. attended a private school. In 2012, as she was finishing ninth grade at the private school, the DOE "held an individualized education program (IEP) meeting to determine the special education services Rachel would receive in the upcoming school year … and proposed placement for her tenth-grade year." DOE proposed that Rachel be placed at Kalani High School for the tenth-grade. Her parents objected; they wanted Rachel to continue at the private school. Later the family moved. They requested the name and location of the proposed high school and repeated their request for a private school placement. The father filed for a due process hearing, alleging that the DOE "denied Rachel a FAPE by not identifying the anticipated school where Rachel's IEP would be implemented. He did not raise any substantive challenge to Rachel's IEP." The DOE claimed that her "IEP could 'be implemented on a public school campus.'" The Hearing Officer agreed. The parents appealed to the U.S. District Court which held that "an IEP need not necessarily identify a specific school where it would be implemented to comply with the IDEA. … [L]ocation does not necessarily include the specific school where special education services will be implemented." Outcome: Hawaii prevailed.

9/13/2017	9th HI	**R.E.B. v. Hawaii DOE** 870 F.3d 1025	This private school tuition reimbursement case includes legal issues related to mootness, transition, IEP specificity, and ABA methodology. Hawaii DOE wanted to move the child from the Pacific Autism Center into public school kindergarten. The parent objected and raised issues about the proposed IEP, LRE, transition, and failure to include ABA methodology. The HO and U.S. District Court held that the public school's proposed IEP was appropriate. The Ninth Circuit reviewed argument raised by the father, reviewed the IEP, and agreed with the father. The transition plan was inadequate, LRE was not specific, and ABA methodology should have been written into the IEP. Reversed and remanded. Initial Outcome: Parent prevailed. However, Hawaii DOE filed a Petition for a Panel Rehearing. On April 3, 2018, the "Opinion and dissent filed on September 13, 2017, are withdrawn, and this case is resubmitted pending further order of this court."
10/2/2017	11th AL	**J.S. v. Houston County Bd. Ed.**	**Wrightslaw Case of the Year** We urge all special education attorneys to read this case. A child with "severe physical disabilities and cognitive impairments" was abused by his aide / paraprofessional who regularly removed J.S. from the classroom and took him to the school's weight room. The child "with some frequency, [was] excluded and isolated from his classroom and peers on the basis of his disability." The Alabama parents filed Section 504 and ADA claims against the Houston County Board of Education alleging abuse of their child. The U.S. District Court dismissed the case "mischaracterizing his Title II and § 504 claim regarding his removal from his regular classroom as merely a claim that he was denied a FAPE, a right guaranteed under the IDEA." The Court of Appeals reversed portions of the decision and remanded it back. The School Board may face a civil Jury Trial for violations of Section 504 and ADA. Outcome: Parents prevailed.

10/10/2017	2nd NY	***N.B. v. NYC DOE***	In this case, the parents rejected a public school "P369K" placement for their child with autism and sought tuition reimbursement for a private school that provided DIR/Floortime as the "means of achieving progress."
			In an unusual decision, the Administrative Hearing Officer (IHO) "found that any procedural defects in developing the IEP were *de minimis,* but that N.B. was denied a FAPE because the Department had failed to offer the IEP into evidence at the hearing. The IHO nonetheless found that the Parents lacked standing to seek tuition reimbursement because "their contract with the private school was illusory."
			The DOE and the parents appealed the IHO's ruling to an SRO. The SRO determined that the IEP was sufficient and offered a FAPE.
			The parents appealed to the U.S. District Court, lost, and appealed to the 2nd Circuit.
			"The SRO reasonably rejected the assertion that DIR/Floortime is the only means of achieving progress such that the IEP's failure to mandate DIR/Floortime amounts to a denial of a FAPE."
			The Second Circuit affirmed the U.S. District Court ruling in favor of the school district.
			Outcome: School prevailed.
10/11/2017	3rd PA Krause	***H.E. v. Walter Palmer Charter Sch. + PA DOE*** 873 F.3d 406	This is a convoluted attorneys' fee case with some legal similarities to the Third Circuit's decision in *M.R. v. Ridley* (8/22/2017) that was authored by the same Judge. The facts are quite different.
			The parents' three children were initially enrolled in a Charter School that failed to provide the children with FAPE.
			The parents filed due process complaints against the Charter School and the Pennsylvania Department of Education (PA DOE). The Hearing Officer dismissed the complaints.
			The parents filed suit in the U.S. District Court against the Charter School and PA DOE and "obtained all of the relief they had sought."
			The parents then filed for attorneys' fees and the District Court "denied the motion, explaining that its grant of summary judgment ... was confined to purely procedural matters ... and that the parents were not prevailing parties."
			Parents appealed to the Court of Appeals which held, "Plaintiffs contend that they in fact were prevailing

			parties for purposes of the IDEA's attorneys' fees provision and that they therefore were eligible for a fee award. Our precedent compels us to agree ..." The Court of Appeals reversed and remanded the case back to the U.S. District Court to determine and calculate the fees to be awarded to the parents. Outcome: Parents prevailed.
12/1/2017	2nd NY	*R.C. v. Bd. Ed. Wappingers Cent. Sch. Dist.*	This is a tuition reimbursement case with conflicting decisions from the IHO and the SRO. The IHO ruled in favor of the parents. The SRO reversed the decision. The parents appealed to the U.S. District Court, lost, and appealed to the Second Circuit. The Second Circuit provided the legal analysis to assess conflicting rulings between an IHO and SRO. The Court also provided the analytical steps in the *Burlington/Carter* test to determine if tuition reimbursement to the parents is justified. The Court of Appeals affirmed the ruling of the U.S. District Court against the parents. Outcome: School district prevailed.
12/8/2017	4th MD Wynn	*N.P. v. Prince George's County Bd. Ed. + Maxwell*	This tuition reimbursement case was directly affected, in mid-stream, by the U.S. Supreme Court ruling in *Endrew F.* issued on March 22, 2017. The Fourth Circuit was quite critical of the U.S. District Court Judge: "The district court ... reversed the ALJ based on the record from the administrative proceedings. The school system timely appealed to this Court." "We need not fully explore the impact of *Endrew* in this case, however. Both the ALJ and the district court wrote their opinions prior to *Endrew*. In fact, the ALJ quotes the 'more than *de minimis*' standard in her opinion. The ALJ—the only person to see the witnesses testify in person—should have the opportunity to decide in the first instance whether the outcome of the case is different under the standard articulated by the Supreme Court in *Endrew*. We therefore remand to the district court so it can order further proceedings consistent with this opinion." Outcome: A draw. Remanded back to the U.S. District Court to reconsider the case in light of the SCOTUS decision in *Endrew*.

12/12/2017	3rd PA Shwartz	*Wellman v. Butler Area Sch. Dist.*	This is a failure to exhaust administrative remedies case based on the SCOTUS *Fry* decision issued on February 22, 2017. The child "suffered a head injury while playing flag football" at school. This injury was compounded by several more concussions at school which resulted in academic problems, "significant stress, embarrassment, and anxiety." The child's mother requested that he be evaluated for an IEP. The school determined that the child was not eligible for an IEP but proposed a Section 504 Plan. The parents placed him in a private school from which he graduated. After their child graduated, the parents sued the "School district and the high school's principal" alleging violations of Section 504 and the ADA. The U.S. District Court dismissed the Complaint. The parents appealed to the Third Circuit which explained "What matters is the crux— or, in legal speak, the gravamen—of the plaintiff's complaint." "Application of the *Fry* framework to Wellman's entire complaint and each of his claims shows that his grievances all stem from the alleged failure to accommodate his condition and fulfill his educational needs ... he cannot cure the defect in his complaint." The Court of Appeals ordered that the Complaint be dismissed with prejudice. Outcome: School district prevailed.
12/19/2017	2nd NY	*J.P. v. NYC DOE*	In a tuition reimbursement case, the parents argued that the DOE failed to conduct an adequate FBA or develop a BIP, that the "public school placement under the IEP was predetermined, impeding their opportunity to meaningfully participate in the decision-making process." The parents lost at due process, at review, and before the U.S. District Court. On appeal, the Second Circuit held, "the IHO's and SRO's decisions merit deference because they are well reasoned and supported by the record … Although the failure to conduct an FBA or BIP in conformity with New York State regulations is a serious procedural violation, it does not rise to the level of a denial of a FAPE if the IEP adequately identifies the problem behavior and prescribes ways to manage it." The Court affirmed the judgment of the U.S. District Court. Outcome: School prevailed.

Chapter 5. Summaries of Decisions

January 1, 2017 through December 31, 2017

This Chapter includes comprehensive summaries of special education decisions in 2017.

Understanding and digesting the full text of a federal court opinion at the U.S. District Court or the U.S. Court of Appeals level can be a slow, cumbersome process. Typically, you must read a case more than once to develop a true understanding of the issues and final outcome of the case.

Although it is easier to read a summary written by someone else, the author's words may reflect that person's biases and may not rely on the Court's words in the decision. If you rely on another person's summary, your understanding of a case will be limited by that individual's understanding. In this Chapter, we keep interpretations to a minimum and provide direct quotes from the court's opinion.

On another note, legal decisions contain numerous references to statutes, regulations, and other cases. These references, known as "citations," provide you with the specific legal authority, including the statute, i.e., United States Code [20 U.S.C. §1400], the federal special education regulation in the Code of Federal Regulations [34 C.F.R. § 300.1], prior U.S. Court of Appeals decisions, and Opinions from the U.S. Supreme Court (SCOTUS). Citations within a decision may take up several lines of text, so we omitted these citations and inserted the phrase "Citation omitted."

In most decisions, Courts of Appeals will quote other cases, testimony, or exhibits used at trial. Typically, Courts of Appeals will provide the citation, i.e. the source of that other quote. However, for visual and reading clarity, we deliberately omitted apostrophes, parentheses and brackets so the full quote is easier to read and understand. If you want to use legal language you see in these cases, find and use language from the original decision issued by the Court.

Earlier in this book you learned how to use "Google Scholar" to find the full text of cases. When you use Google Scholar, you can also find the earlier U.S. District Court decision(s) that triggered an appeal to the Court of Appeals.

Role of the Council of Parent Attorneys and Advocates (COPAA)

In 1998, we were involved in founding a new organization, the Council of Parent Attorneys and Advocates (COPAA) (www.copaa.org). Over the years COPAA submitted Amicus Briefs to the U.S. Court of Appeals and to SCOTUS (*Fry* and *Endrew F.*) and has an 80% record of success. At the end of each case, we provide you with the names of the attorneys and indicate those cases where COPAA submitted an Amicus Brief.

A.M. v. NYC DOE
2nd Cir.

Circuit Judge Wesley

1/10/2017 – New York

In this tuition reimbursement / ABA methodology case, the parents lost at the Due Process Hearing, lost at the Review Hearing, and lost at the U.S. District Court. The IHO, SRO, and District Court judge primarily relied on the testimony "from O'Sullivan, the DOE school psychologist who also served as the DOE representative on the CSE that formulated the terms of E.H.'s IEP."

In the Second Circuit's reversal, the Court noted that "O'Sullivan never actually met or evaluated E.H. until after the formulation of his IEP, a violation of New York law."

"The SRO reviewed the evaluative materials present at the CSE meeting and the IHO hearing record, and concluded, relying heavily on O'Sullivan's testimony, that the IEP was substantively adequate despite the absence of any provision for 1:1 ABA therapy because, although the May 2012 CSE did not recommend ABA, it also did not disapprove of the methodology or say ABA should not be used with the student, and that the IEP incorporated behavioral methodologies ... not contrary to ABA."

"The District Court credited O'Sullivan's IHO hearing testimony that the DOE deliberately formulated the IEP in this manner because it 'didn't want to tie the hands of the different disciplines that would be working with E.H. by requiring a specific methodology for part or all of the day.'"

"The District Court and administrative officers' reliance on the views of O'Sullivan, which were against the clear consensus of the substance of the evaluative materials present at the CSE meeting

and the views of E.H.'s evaluators and educational instructors i.e., all witnesses familiar with E.H., was error, as this resulted in a proposed program that

was not 'reasonably calculated to enable E.H. to receive educational benefits. [Citation omitted.] This conclusion is inescapable, 'particularly when combined with (1) the [DOE's] failure to [conduct] an adequate, individualized [FBA], (2) the DOE's failure to prepare an adequate BIP, (3) the lack of any provision for parent counseling and training, and (4) the omission of transitional support services in the IEP for E.H.'s would-be public school teacher at the IEP's proposed placement." [Citation omitted.]

"Moreover, we note that the issue of classroom placement ratio cannot be separated from one of the procedural violations discussed above, namely the [DOE's] failure to [evaluate E.H. and] conduct an appropriate [FBA of its own] or [BIP]. Id. Indeed, we are left to wonder whether the DOE would have reached the same conclusions and recommended the same deficient services in the IEP that E.H.'s evaluators and instructors believed to be inadequate, had the DOE adequately complied with the IDEA's procedures in the first instance." [Citation omitted.]

"Accordingly, we conclude that these significant deficiencies rendered E.H.'s IEP for the 2012-2013 school year substantively inadequate, thereby depriving E.H. of a FAPE."

(**Wrightslaw Note**: COPAA filed an Amicus Brief on behalf of the parents.)

(Parent's Attorney – Jason H. Stern (Cuddy Law Firm) // School's Attorney – Aaron M. Bloom // COPAA Amicus Attorney – Andrew A. Feinstein)

Outcome: Reversed and remanded. Parents prevailed.

L.K. v. NYC DOE
2nd Cir.
1/19/2017 – New York

In this tuition reimbursement case, the parents were seeking full reimbursement for private school tuition and supplemental services. The parents' appeal was based on the third prong of the *Burlington/Carter* test.

(**Wrightslaw Note**: The *Burlington/Carter* test is based on two SCOTUS decisions. *Burlington* is the 1985 case that authorized reimbursement to parents for private school tuition if the public school failed to provide FAPE. *Carter* is the author's 1993 SCOTUS case that expanded on *Burlington*.)

The parents also argued "that the DOE's rate of reimbursement was too low to sufficiently reimburse them because it did not take into account New York City market rates for L.K.'s services providers."

"[T]he Parents' argument that they are entitled to full reimbursement once a program is found to be appropriate under the second prong misunderstands the *Burlington/Carter* test that this court must apply."

"[T]otal reimbursement is appropriate where the cost is reasonable, even where the cost is more than it might have cost the state to provide the service in the first place. This is because public educational authorities who want to avoid reimbursing parents for the private education of a disabled child can do one of two things: give the child a FAPE in a public setting, or place the child in an appropriate private setting of the state's choice."

The Court upheld denial of private tuition but remanded the case back to the U.S. District Court to determine the amount and extent of reimbursement for the supplemental OT services.

(**Wrightslaw Note:** COPAA filed an Amicus Brief on behalf of the parents.)

(Parent's Attorney – Gary S. Mayerson // School's Attorney – Emma Grunberg // COPAA Amicus Attorney – Andrew A. Feinstein)

Outcome: School prevailed on most, but not all issues. Remanded for further proceedings.

M. v. Falmouth Sch. Dept.
1st Cir.
847 F.3d 19
Circuit Judge Stahl
1/27/2017 - Maine

In this case, the parent asserted "that her daughter's IEP specified that Falmouth would instruct O.M. using the Specialized Program Individualizing Reading Excellence (SPIRE) system during her third-grade year. She insists that this system constituted a key provision of O.M.'s IEP and, because Falmouth did not provide O.M. with SPIRE instruction, the School Department therefore violated her daughter's right to a FAPE. Falmouth, for its part, counters that O.M.'s IEP does not mention SPIRE and that any references to it were relegated to ancillary documents which should not be read into the IEP or made a part of the IEP."

In a footnote, the Court explained that "SPIRE" is a teacher directed, systematic, multisensory, synthetic phonics literacy instructional program" based, in part, on the Orton-Gillingham Approach.

"After an administrative hearing and a magistrate judge's review of that hearing, the district court agreed with Ms. M. and entered judgment in her favor. However, after careful review we reach a contrary conclusion and find that O.M.'s IEP did not mandate that Falmouth use SPIRE, meaning the School Department neither breached the IEP's terms nor denied O.M. a FAPE by foregoing such instruction. Accordingly, we reverse."

Initially, the parent initially objected to SPIRE and requested a Due Process Hearing. SPIRE was not included in the IEP and the school district discontinued its use. Later, the parent filed a DP request, alleging that the district failed to use SPIRE, which was noted in the Prior Written Notice, but not included in the IEP. The Court explained that "Written Prior Notice is meant to spell out more specific, but not binding, proposals for implementing that [IEP] framework."

The Court concluded "that Falmouth complied with the terms of O.M.'s IEP and committed no IDEA violation."

(Parent's Attorney – Richard L. O'Meara // School's Attorney – Eric R. Herlan)

Outcome: School prevailed.

J.D. v. NYC DOE
2nd Cir.
1/27/2017 – New York

In this tuition reimbursement case, the parents argued that the 2011 IEP was not appropriate. The IHO and SRO disagreed and denied tuition reimbursement. On appeal, the Circuit Court analyzed the 2011 IEP and found that it "was substantially similar to the 2010 version that the IHO found to be inadequate, except for several additional recommendations, most notable of which was the supplemental Special Education Teacher Support Services (SETSS) instruction. The pertinent issue then, is whether inclusion of the SETSS sessions was sufficient to render the 2011 IEP adequate."

As a sixth grader, A.P. was a non-reader for whom intense reading instruction was recommended. Initially, he was in the public school program, then the school district placed him in the "Sterling School, a specialized private school for children with language-based learning disabilities. For the remainder of the sixth grade, Sterling placed A.P. in classes with a ratio of nine students to two teachers, and provided him with additional one-on-one

instruction throughout the day. By May 2011, A.P. was reading at a mid-first grade level."

For the next school year, the school district proposed returning him to public school, but his mother objected arguing "the prescribed SETSS sessions would not have been sufficiently intense to provide A.P. with educational benefits. The 2011 IEP provided for five 45-minute SETSS sessions per week (compared to the Evaluation's recommended 90-minute sessions four or five times a week) in instructional groups of up to eight students (whereas the Evaluation recommended no more than three students in a group)." The parent kept her son at Sterling and sued for tuition reimbursement.

In reversing the lower decisions, the Second Circuit stated: "We neither know, nor have an opinion as to, the number of hours of SETSS that would have been appropriate for A.P., or whether group sizes of eight or three would be needed to provide him with an educational benefit. We admittedly lack the 'specialized knowledge and educational expertise' necessary to make such pedagogical determinations." [Citation omitted.]

"To meet its burden to show the appropriateness of the IEP, however, the DOE needed more than conclusory and contradictory testimony from its witnesses. [Citation omitted.] The SRO and IHO also needed to address the intensity question in light of the Evaluation and A.P.'s progress at Sterling and provide reasons for their conclusion that the SETSS sessions were adequate. We therefore hold that a preponderance of the evidence does not support the IHO and SRO's determination that the 2011 IEP would have provided A.P. with a FAPE."

(Parent's Attorney – Caroline J. Heller // School's Attorney – Max McCann // COPAA Amicus Attorney – Carl H. Loewenson, Jr.)

Outcome: Parent prevailed. The Court reversed the U.S. District Court and remanded it back.

Luo v. Baldwin Union Free Sch. Dist.
2nd Cir.
1/27/2017 – New York

In this "collateral estoppel" case, the parents represented themselves in regard to an earlier litigated case about the child's placement "at a particular out-of-state school for the 2011-2012 school year."

"It is well settled, however, that the IDEA does not authorize parents to determine the 'bricks and mortar' of the specific school."

In this new case involving the same parties and same issue, the Court explained that "Under the doctrine of collateral estoppel, a litigant is prevented from relitigating in a subsequent action an issue of fact or law that was fully and fairly litigated in a prior proceeding."

The parents also objected that the school district was permitted to file a late answer and was not held in default. In response, the Court explained that "The district court considered the appropriate factors, and its conclusion that Baldwin and Gallo established excusable neglect for their failure timely to answer the complaint due to confusion from Luo's multiple pending actions and motion for reconsideration falls within the range of permissible decisions."

(Parent's Attorney – Pro Se // School's Attorney – Kelly E. Wright)

Outcome: Case dismissed. School prevailed.

Issa v. Lancaster Sch. Dist.
3rd Cir.
847 F.3d 121
Circuit Judge Fisher
1/30/2017 - Pennsylvania

Non-English-speaking immigrant school-age refugees were placed into Phoenix Academy, an alternative education program "intended to serve at-risk Students over-age for their grade, under-credited, and in danger of not graduating high school before they age out of public-school eligibility at 21."

Several organizations sued on behalf of the children under the Equal Educational Opportunities Act of 1974 (EEOA), 20 U.S.C. § 1703(f) seeking a preliminary injunction ordering placement into "McCaskey High School's International School, a program designed principally to teach language skills to English language learners, or ELLs."

The U.S. District Court granted the Preliminary Injunction and the School District appealed to the Court of Appeals.

On appeal, the Third Circuit explained that the "named plaintiffs, now the appellees, are immigrants, ages 18 to 21. They fled war, violence, and persecution in their native countries to come to the United States, arriving here since 2014. International refugee agencies resettled them in Lancaster, Pennsylvania. None are native English speakers. As students, all fall within a subgroup of ELLs called SLIFE—students with limited or interrupted formal education. SLIFE are English language learners who are two or more years behind their appropriate grade level, possess limited or no literacy in any language, have limited or interrupted formal educational backgrounds, and have endured stressful experiences causing acculturation challenges. The named plaintiffs embody these traits."

The Court queried: "How does the School District empirically evaluate the efficacy of Phoenix's ESL program? It doesn't. The School District does not assess in any measurable way whether Phoenix's program helps ELLs overcome their language barriers. It hasn't attempted to weigh concretely the impact Phoenix's accelerated, non-sheltered program has on ELLs, including SLIFE."

The Court applied a four-factor test to determine whether there was a violation of 20 U.S.C. § 1703(f) - "(1) the defendant must be an educational agency,

(2) the plaintiff must face language barriers impeding her equal participation in the defendant's instructional programs, (3) the defendant must have failed to take appropriate action to overcome those barriers, and (4) the plaintiff must have been denied equal educational opportunity on account of her race, color, sex, or national origin. See 20 U.S.C. § 1703(f); id. § 1720(a) (defining 'educational agency')."

The Court discussed each element: With the last the Court explained that: "We now address §1703(f)'s fourth and final element, which requires proof the plaintiffs were denied equal educational opportunity on account of their race, color, sex, or national origin. See 20 U.S.C. § 1703(f). We hold they met this element."

"[T]hey were denied equal educational opportunity on account of an EEOA-protected characteristic: their national origins."

(Parent's Attorney – Witold J. Walczak // School's Attorney – Thomas A. Specht)

Outcome: The Court of Appeals affirmed the ruling in favor of the students.

Fry v. Napoleon Comm. Sch.

U.S. Supreme Court

Unanimous 9-0

Justice Kagan

2/22/2017

(**Wrightslaw Note**: This the landmark "Exhaustion of Administrative Remedies" case.)

Ehlena Fry has a severe type of cerebral palsy that affects her legs, arms, and body. Below are some of the facts of the case as taken from the Petition for Certiorari.

"In 2009, when she was five years old, E.F. obtained a service dog prescribed by her pediatrician to help her live as independently as possible ... E.F's pediatrician and family intended to have Wonder accompany E.F. at all times to facilitate her independence and ensure that she and Wonder would bond after training."

"In October 2009, Ehlena's parents acquired Wonder, a Goldendoodle that was specially trained to help Ehlena with balance, retrieve dropped items, open and close doors, turn on lights and perform many other tasks. Wonder is hypoallergenic and is trained to stay out of the way when he is not working."

"Respondents Napoleon Community Schools and Jackson County Intermediate School District refused to permit E.F. to attend school with her service dog ... As a result, E.F. was forced to attend school without her prescribed service dog from October 2009 to April 2010."

After months of mediation, the school allowed Wonder to accompany Ehlena for a 'trial period' but did not allow Wonder to work. Instead, "[T]he school required the dog to remain in the back of the room during classes, forbade the dog from assisting E.F. with many tasks he had been trained to do, and banned the dog from accompanying and assisting her during recess, lunch, computer lab, library time and other activities. After the trial period, the School District refused to permit Wonder to accompany E.F. to school."

The parents brought suit under the ADA and Section 504 of the Rehabilitation Act (504), not under The Individuals with Disabilities Education Act (IDEA).

In the earlier decision (*Fry v. Napoleon*, 788 F.3d 622 (6th Cir. 2015)), the Court of Appeals for the Sixth Circuit upheld a ruling by a Michigan federal court that Ehlena Fry's parents were required to request a special education due process hearing, i.e., exhaust their administrative remedies, before they could file suit for monetary damages under the ADA and Section 504. This ruling widened a split among circuits about requiring parents to exhaust administrative remedies under IDEA, even though the relief they sought was not available under the IDEA.

In *Fry,* SCOTUS ruled in favor of the parents, holding that, under her facts, exhaustion of administrative procedures was not necessary, explaining that you have to look at the "gravamen" the essence of the case, to see if the remedy the parent sought was or was not truly educational in nature.

"In determining whether a plaintiff seeks relief for the denial of a FAPE, what matters is the gravamen of the plaintiff's complaint, setting aside any attempts at artful pleading. That inquiry makes central the plaintiff's own claims, as §1415(l) explicitly requires in asking whether a lawsuit in fact seeks relief available under the IDEA. But examination of a plaintiff's complaint should consider substance, not surface: §1415(l) requires exhaustion when the gravamen of a complaint seeks redress for a school's failure to provide a FAPE, even if not phrased or framed in precisely that way."

This unanimous decision from the U.S. Supreme Court is a landmark case. At the end of our summary, we have links to the full text of the *Fry* Opinion, the Syllabus of the case that was issued by the Reporter of Decisions and the transcript of Justice Kagan's Announcement of the Opinion when, in her own words, she summarized the essence of the case.

(**Wrightslaw Note**: In the history of special education case law where the sole issue was the failure to exhaust administrative remedies, co-author, Peter W. D. Wright, had one of the first cases. See *McGovern v. Sullins*, 676 F.2d 98 (4th Cir. 1982) in which both counsel and the parties agreed that exhaustion would be futile and was not legally required. Regardless, the District Court Judge, *sua sponte*, on his own motion, dismissed the case, which was upheld by the Fourth Circuit.)

(Parent's Attorney – Samuel R. Bagenstos and James F. Hermon // School's Attorney – Neal Kumar Katyal // COPAA Attorney – Selene Almazan-Altobelli)

Outcome: Parents prevailed. On remand, there have been several unsuccessful settlement conferences between the parties. In a March 19, 2018 Motion for Summary Judgment, the school district argued that the Frys were seeking educational relief, thus they did not exhaust their IDEA remedies. On June 7, 2018, newly appointed District Court Judge Cox will hold a Hearing in regard to the pending Motions. From the Court's Docket Sheet, it appears that discovery has completed.

Below are links to the Syllabus, the Full Text of the Decision and Justice Kagan's remarks when the decision was announced from the bench.

Reyes v. Manor Indep. Sch. Dist.
5th Cir.
850 F.3d 251
Circuit Judge Costa
3/7/2017 - Texas

After their son, E.M., turned 18, the parent filed a request for a due process hearing. E.M. has "severe intellectual disabilities and autism, with psychiatric evaluations placing his developmental age at around three years old."

In this Statute of Limitations (SOL), "tolling" and failure to exhaust administrative remedies case, the court explained that "Parents are given the authority to enforce their child's IDEA rights, but that authority transfers to the child when he turns 18."

The parents did not have the legal "capacity to file suit on behalf of her son" until they later "obtained a state court order finding E.M. incompetent and appointing them to be his guardian." Afterwards they refiled and the case was litigated. The essence of the case was related to relief that was available under IDEA.

The Hearing Officer, the U.S. District Court, and Court of Appeals found that "most of the IDEA claims fell outside the one-year [SOL] window." Relying upon *Fry* "[t]he district court was correct in holding that E.M. failed to exhaust his Rehabilitation Act claims by only pleading those claims, because he did not address them in his prehearing request for relief or otherwise obtain any decision on them from the hearing officer." "In any event, E.M.'s Rehabilitation Act claims overlap with his IDEA claims."

(**Wrightslaw Note**: This case was reissued on May 11, 2017 with slight editing of citations and a clarification about "tolling," noting that the SOL begins when the plaintiff "knew or should have known" about the claim or injury.)

(Parent's Attorney – Yvonnilda Garza Muniz // School's Attorney – Todd Aaron Clark)

Outcome: School prevailed.

J.M. v. Francis Howell Sch. Dist.
8th Cir.
850 F.3d 944
Circuit Judge Benton
3/7/2017 – Missouri

On behalf of her son, J.M. the parent filed suit in the U.S. District Court under federal law and the state's Missouri Human Rights Act (MHRA) alleging "unlawful use of isolation and physical restraints."

"McCauley alleges that between January 2012 and September 2014, J.M. repeatedly was placed in physical restraints and isolation without her knowledge. Learning of this, she immediately contacted the District, requesting restraints only when necessary and no isolation. On September 5, McCauley removed J.M. from the District."

"McCauley did not file an IDEA due process complaint, request a due process hearing, or engage in the exhaustion procedures under the IDEA."

"McCauley sued in federal court under the IDEA, 42 U.S.C. §§ 1983 and 1988, and Missouri common law (torts of negligence per se, false imprisonment, and battery). She amended the complaint to add claims under the ADA and MHRA. The District answered, claiming failure to exhaust administrative remedies for the federal claims, and sovereign immunity for the common law tort claims. McCauley voluntarily amended her complaint, removing the IDEA and common law tort claims."

Prior to the SCOTUS *Fry* ruling, the U.S. District Court dismissed because the parents failed to exhaust administrative remedies. Two weeks after the SCOTUS *Fry* decision, the Eighth Circuit analyzed this appeal. Pursuant to *Fry*, the plaintiff argued that "exhaustion is not required because she does not seek relief available under the IDEA."

The Eighth Circuit explained that "There are three exceptions to the exhaustion requirement: (1) futility, (2) 'inability of the administrative remedies to provide adequate relief,' and (3) 'the establishment of an agency policy or practice of general applicability that is contrary to law.'"

In light of *Fry*, the Court explained that: "The IDEA's exhaustion requirement also applies to claims under the Constitution, the ADA, the Rehabilitation Act, and other federal laws protecting children with disabilities to the extent those claims seek relief 'that is also available under [the IDEA].'"

"McCauley also claims the administrative process would not have addressed all her claims. This, however, does not excuse exhaustion. Although the administrative process may not address all claims, this court has held exhaustion is not futile because it would allow 'the agency to develop the record for judicial review and apply its expertise' to the plaintiff's 'claims to the extent those claims are related to implementation' of the IEP."

"McCauley contends the administrative process cannot provide adequate relief, compensatory and punitive damages. As discussed, this argument is without merit. IDEA's exhaustion requirement remains the general rule, regardless of whether the administrative process offers the particular type of relief that is being sought."

(**Wrightslaw Note**: Even though it was known that the *Fry* case was pending before SCOTUS, the Eighth Circuit held Oral Argument on January 10, 2017. The *Fry* decision was issued by SCOTUS on February 22, 2017. On March 5, 2017 parent's counsel filed a Motion requesting permission to file a Supplemental Memorandum in light of *Fry*. On March 7 2017, the Motion was denied and this decision was issued that same day. This case was not appealed to SCOTUS.)

(Parent's Attorney – Larry Alan Bagsby // School's Attorney – Cindy Reeds Ormsby)

Outcome: Dismissal upheld, parent failed to exhaust. School prevailed.

S.H. v. Tustin Unif. Sch. Dist.
9th Cir.
3/15/2017 - California

In this proposed change of educational placement case, the district proposed changing the child's "education placement from a program operated by the Orange County Department of Education to a Tustin-run special day class. Tustin made its placement offer ... following the last of six triennial Individualized Education Program (IEP) meetings, but Appellants refused to consent to Tustin's placement offer."

The parents asserted that the district had predetermined the placement, failed to provide proper "Prior Written Notice" and failed to "adequately involve" the parents in arriving at the placement decision.

"Tustin and Appellants separately filed due process actions. An Administrative Law Judge (ALJ) for the California Office of Administrative Hearings consolidated the cases and held hearings over six days, receiving evidence and hearing testimony from twelve witnesses involved in S.H.'s IEP process. The ALJ ultimately held that Tustin would provide S.H. with a free appropriate public education (FAPE) and therefore Tustin could go forward with the placement. The district court granted summary judgment in favor of Tustin."

The Ninth Circuit upheld the ALJ and the U.S. District Court's approval of the school district's proposed change of placement. They also found that the parents participated in the decision process and the school did not predetermine the placement.

(Attorney information not provided by Google.)

Outcome: District decision affirmed. School prevailed.

Ostby v. Manhattan Sch. Dist.
7th Cir.
851 F.3d 677
Circuit Judge Rovner
3/16/2017 – Illinois

This concerns a case becoming "moot" with a continuation of ongoing litigation *vis a vis* the "Stay Put" statute.

Jacob had an IEP and was enrolled in the public school's "general education kindergarten classroom with social emotional services and resource support."

"[A]fter additional testing, the Ostbys and the psychologist they hired to evaluate Jacob met with the District to develop a new IEP. As a result of that meeting, some of Jacob's services were discontinued and a Behavioral Intervention Plan was adopted. The District also recommended that

Jacob's placement be changed from the general education setting to the Social Emotional Learning Foundations program (SELF program). Jacob's parents objected to the SELF program placement and it was not adopted at that time."

Later, "the District sought to place Jacob in the SELF program over his parents' objections. The SELF program is a restricted form of education that is not part of a mainstream classroom. Moreover, the SELF program was housed at a different school in a different school district. One goal of the Act is to educate disabled children in the least restrictive environment ... Jacob's parents believed that the SELF program was more restrictive than necessary and that he should remain in the general education setting in his home district."

"There was a six-day administrative hearing in August and September 2014, and, in a 38-page decision dated September 22, 2014, the hearing officer found for the School District on every issue but one." At the U.S. District Court appeal, the parents also lost on every issue except one, an award of $3,126.10 for a private evaluation. The U.S. District Court in the published decision at 173 F. Supp. 3d 744 explained that "Stay Put" is to "freeze a child's educational placement during the pendency of due process proceedings." [Citation omitted.]

That District Court stated: "More recently, the parties also reported to this Court that, apart from the issues asserted here (such as financial reimbursement), a general consensus is thankfully emerging among the parties regarding Jacob's placement and educational plan going forward."

When Oral Argument was held at the Seventh Circuit, the school "nevertheless continues to defend its decision to place Jacob in the SELF program for first grade. And even though they have now agreed to a new IEP for third grade, the Ostbys continue to challenge the District's decision to place Jacob in the SELF program in first grade."

"The District and the Ostbys have reached an agreement regarding Jacob's IEP and his placement in general education for third grade, and the District has no pending proposal to move Jacob to the SELF program."

Pursuant to "Stay Put" the child was never placed into the SELF program and continuously remained in the general education program. The only remaining issue was the cost of parent's legal representation and whether the school district would have to pay attorneys' fees to the parents as prevailing parties.

While the parents may have prevailed in fact, they did not prevail in the Courtroom, so could they recover their attorneys' fees? The Seventh Circuit provided a comprehensive analysis about continuing jurisdiction to hear a case and that "The parties must continue to have a personal stake in the outcome of the lawsuit."

"[A] case becomes moot when a court's decision can no longer affect the rights of litigants in the case and simply would be an opinion advising what the law would be upon a hypothetical state of facts."

"Once a case is moot, we cannot consider the merits of the district court's decision to determine whether the parents are prevailing parties for the purpose of assessing attorneys' fees."

"The Ostbys did not prevail before the district court and we may not consider the merits of that decision solely for the purpose of determining their entitlement to attorneys' fees."

"There is no longer an injury that can be redressed by a favorable decision" and the appeal was dismissed with instructions to the U.S. District Court "to dismiss it as moot." (Parents were able to recover the private evaluation costs.)

(Parent's Attorney – Pamela R. Cleary // School's Attorney – Laura Sinars)
Outcome: Case is now moot. School prevailed.

E.F. v. Newport Mesa Unif. Sch. Dist.

9th Cir.

3/21/2017 – California

This case is about the "deference" provided when a case is on appeal. When a case is appealed, "deference" is provided to the rulings issued by the prior, lower level Judges and Hearing Officers.

Typically, a U.S. District Court Judge does not hear new evidence, but instead reviews the lower level decision and may review testimony, exhibits, transcripts and briefs.

The Ninth Circuit's decision did not provide any background about the facts of this case. It was necessary to review the U.S. District Court's Opinion to understand the history.

The U.S. District Court noted that: "At the time the OAH Decision was issued in December 26, 2013, E.F. was a seven-year-old boy who resided within the jurisdictional boundaries of the Newport-Mesa Unified School District in California. E.F. is a child with autism and suffers from cognitive and communication delays. The District placed E.F. in the special education program in February 2009."

After an unsuccessful due process hearing, the parents appealed the case to the U.S. District Court. The decision in Case No. SACV 14-00455-CJC(RNBx) was issued by the U.S. District Court Judge Carney on June 22, 2015.

He explained that the "Plaintiffs due process request was ultimately heard over a seven-day hearing before the ALJ in October 2013. After receiving approximately 50 documents into evidence and hearing testimony from 16 witnesses ... and the Parents, the ALJ found that Plaintiffs had failed to meet their burden of proof that the goals set by the District, E.F.'s placement, and most services in E.F.'s IEPs were legally inadequate. The ALJ further found that Plaintiffs failed to demonstrate that the District's assessments were improper or that the District staff was not properly

trained to provide E.F. with instruction or services."

Judge Carney discussed each issue raised by the parents and noted that "The ALJ found that Plaintiffs had failed to meet their burden of proof that the goals set by the District, E.F.'s placement, and most services in E.F.'s IEPs were legally inadequate. The ALJ further found that Plaintiffs failed to demonstrate that the District's assessments were improper or that the District staff was not properly trained to provide E.F. with instruction or services."

The Ninth Circuit stated that "It was proper for the district court to accord the ALJ's decision substantial deference, because the ALJ's decision was thorough, careful, impartial, and sensitive to the complexity of the issues presented. The ALJ's sixty-one-page decision contained findings of fact sufficiently linked to discrete analysis and thoughtful consideration of the documents and testimony received during the seven-day administrative hearing."

(Attorney information not provided by Google.)

Initial Outcome: School prevailed. The U.S. District Court decision was upheld by Ninth Circuit.

The *Endrew F.* SCOTUS decision was issued one day after their unsuccessful outcome. The parents filed a Petition for Certiorari with SCOTUS on June 23, 2017. Certiorari was granted on October 2, 2017. SCOTUS vacated the Ninth Circuit's judgment and remanded for reconsideration in light of its opinion in *Endrew F. v. Douglas Cty. Sch. Dist.* New briefs were filed with the Ninth Circuit. On February 14, 2018 the Court issued a new Opinion that upheld the March 21, 2017 Opinion. The Court noted that "the ALJ's application of the Ninth Circuit's standard was proper even before *Endrew F.* clarified the Supreme Court's holding in *Rowley*."

Final Outcome: School prevailed. The U.S. District Court decision was upheld by Ninth Circuit.

Endrew F. v. Douglas County Sch. Dist.
U.S. Supreme Court
Unanimous 9-0
Chief Justice Roberts
3/22/2017

This appeal was related to the legal definition of FAPE. In 1982, SCOTUS defined the term "free appropriate public education" (FAPE) in the *Rowley* case. **Note**: Unknown to many, Amy Rowley's standardized test scores, as charted out by the District Court Judge, were higher than many of her peers. *Endrew F.* expanded on and partially redefined FAPE.

The Syllabus explains that "Endrew F., a child with autism, received annual IEPs in respondent Douglas County School District from preschool through fourth grade. By fourth grade, Endrew's parents believed his academic and functional progress had stalled. When the school district proposed a fifth grade IEP that resembled those from past years, Endrew's parents removed him from public school and enrolled him in a specialized private school, where he made significant progress."

"School district representatives later presented Endrew's parents with a new fifth grade IEP, but they considered it no more adequate than the original plan. They then sought reimbursement for Endrew's private school tuition by filing a complaint under the IDEA with the Colorado Department of Education. Their claim was denied, and a Federal District Court affirmed that determination. The Tenth Circuit also affirmed."

"That court interpreted *Rowley* to establish a rule that a child's IEP is adequate as long as it is calculated to confer an educational benefit that is merely ... more than de minimis, ... and concluded that Endrew's IEP had been reasonably calculated to enable him to make some progress." The Tenth Circuit held that Endrew had received a FAPE.

The issues between different circuits and subsequent split, revolved around the terms "some educational benefit" versus "meaningful educational benefit."

Chief Justice Roberts noted that the *Rowley* District Court "acknowledged that Amy was making excellent progress in school: She was performing better than the average child in her class' and 'advancing easily from grade to grade."

"The IEP provisions [of IDEA] reflect *Rowley's* expectation that, for most children, a FAPE will involve integration in the regular classroom and individualized special education calculated to achieve advancement from grade to grade."

The *Rowley* decision "had no need to provide concrete guidance with respect to a child who is not fully integrated in the regular classroom and not able to achieve on grade level. That case concerned a young girl who was progressing smoothly through the regular curriculum."

"In view of Amy Rowley's excellent progress and the "substantial" suite of specialized instruction and services offered in her IEP, we concluded that her program satisfied the FAPE requirement."

SCOTUS explained that the old *Rowley* standard is applicable to children with disabilities who are fully integrated in a mainstream, full inclusion setting, but is not necessarily applicable in other settings. This was not a reversal of the 1982 *Rowley* decision, but clarified that a different standard should be used for children with disabilities who are not fully mainstreamed.

"The IEP must aim to enable the child to make progress. After all, the essential function of an IEP is to set out a plan for pursuing academic and functional advancement."

The Court held that "A focus on the particular child is at the core of the IDEA. The instruction offered must be specially designed to meet a child's unique needs through an [i]ndividualized education program. §§1401(29), (14) An IEP is not a form document. It is constructed only after careful consideration of the child's present levels of achievement, disability, and potential for growth. §§1414(d)(1)(A)(i)(I)–(IV), (d)(3)(A)(i)–(iv)."

(**Wrightslaw Note**: The IEP statute, 20 U.S.C. §1414(d), begins on page 99 in *Wrightslaw: Special Education Law, 2nd Ed.*)

"When all is said and done, a student offered an educational program providing merely more than 'de minimis' progress from year to year can hardly be said to have been offered an education at all. For children with disabilities, receiving instruction that aims so low would be tantamount to sitting idly ... awaiting the time when they were old enough to drop out."

"The IDEA demands more. It requires an educational program reasonably calculated to enable a child to make progress appropriate in light of the child's circumstances."

(Parent's Attorney – Jack D. Robinson and Jeffrey L. Fisher // School's Attorney – Neal Kumar Katyal // COPAA Attorney – Caroline J. Heller)

Outcome: Parents prevailed. Per emails and telephone calls with Jack Robinson, and a review of the February 12, 2018 U.S. District Court decision, on remand, that Court issued a strong pro child decision with tuition reimbursement and attorneys' fees to the parents.

Below are links to the Syllabus, the Full Text of the Decision and Chief Justice Roberts remarks when the decision was announced from the bench.
Return to the Table of Decisions

M.C. v Antelope Valley Union High Sch. Dist.
9th Cir.
852 F.3d 840
858 F.3d 1189
Circuit Judge Kozinski
3/27/2017, amended 5/30/2017 – California

This is a **Wrightslaw Case of the Year.** All special education attorneys should read this case because the language relies on *Endrew F:* the focus on the child's potential; that an IEP is much like a contract; the school district's alteration of the IEP without parent's knowledge or consent; the threat of sanctions against a school board attorney regarding whether the attorney attempted to mislead the parents and opposing counsel versus mere bungling; and the school district's failure to file a response to the parents Due Process Complaint Notice.

SCOTUS issued *Endrew F.* on Wednesday, March 22, 2017. Five days later, on Monday the 27th, the Ninth Circuit issued *Antelope Valley,* which relies on *Endrew F.*

About two months later, the Ninth Circuit made slight modifications and re-issued the decision. The initial March 27 version, under Subpart A2, at the bottom of page 10 in the Court's Opinion, stated that "An IEP is a contract." The later May 30 revision deleted that sentence and substituted "An IEP, like a contract, may not be changed unilaterally. It embodies a binding commitment and provides notice to both parties as to what services will be provided to the student during the period covered by the IEP."

In this decision, the Ninth Circuit was quite critical of the ALJ, the U.S. District Court Judge, and School Board Counsel.

As background, "M.C. suffers from Norrie Disease, a genetic disorder that renders him blind. He also has a host of other deficits that cause him developmental delays in all academic areas. M.C.'s mother, M.N., met with several school administrators and instructors to discuss M.C.'s educational challenges and draft an individualized educational program ('IEP'). At the conclusion of this meeting, she signed an IEP document and authorized the goals and services but did not agree it provides a FAPE."

"M.N. then filed a due process complaint alleging that the Antelope Valley Union High School District (the District) committed procedural and substantive violations of the IDEA. The due process hearing took place before an Administrative Law Judge who denied all of M.C.'s claims and the district court affirmed."

"The district court accorded the ALJ's findings substantial deference because the ALJ questioned witnesses during a three-day hearing and wrote a 21-page opinion that reviewed the qualifications of witnesses and culled relevant details from the record. But neither the duration of the hearing, nor the ALJ's active involvement, nor the length of the ALJ's opinion can ensure that the ALJ was thorough and careful." [Citation omitted.]

"We can accord some deference to the ALJ's factual findings, but only where they are thorough and careful, and the extent of deference to be given is within our discretion."

"And, in this case, the ALJ was neither thorough nor careful. As plaintiffs point out, the ALJ didn't address all issues and disregarded some of the evidence presented at the hearing. Even the district court recognized that the ALJ's analysis is not entirely satisfying. Accordingly, the district court erred in deferring to the ALJ's findings." The Ninth Circuit explained that "the district judge must actually examine the record to determine whether it supports the ALJ's opinion."

Unknown to the parent and prior to the due process hearing, Antelope Valley altered the IEP. The mother "didn't learn of it until the first day of the due process hearing, a month later." It appears that the last agreed upon and signed IEP offered 240 minutes of services per month from a Teacher of Visually Impaired (TVI), but the school staff

testified that the amount of services was "per week." "And it turns out that the amendment didn't even provide an accurate statement of the services that M.C. was offered. District witnesses later testified that the District intended to offer M.C. 300 minutes of TVI services per week." The shifting testimony and unilaterally altered IEP concerned the Ninth Circuit.

Because the school district did not "notify M.N. and seek her consent for any amendment ... the IEP actually in force at the time of the hearing was that signed by the parties, not that presented by the District as the amended IEP. Allowing the District to change the IEP unilaterally undermines its function of giving notice of the services the school district has agreed to provide and measuring the student's progress toward the goals outlined in the IEP. Moreover, any such unilateral amendment is a per se procedural violation of the IDEA because it vitiates the parents' right to participate at every step of the IEP drafting process."

"Finally, we must express our disapproval of the District's conduct with respect to this issue. The District discovered what it believed was a mistake in the IEP just a week after it was signed, yet failed to bring this problem to M.N.'s attention until weeks later, on the first day of the due process hearing. Even then, its lawyers didn't identify the purported amendment but rather buried it in a document production, leaving it to plaintiffs' counsel to stumble upon it. Had the District raised the issue immediately upon discovering the suspected error, it's entirely possible that M.N. would have found the amount of TVI services to be satisfactory. Plaintiffs might have avoided hiring a lawyer and taking the case to a due process

The Ninth Circuit directed the U.S. District Court Judge to investigate this issue. "On remand, the district court shall determine whether this course of conduct was a deliberate attempt to mislead M.N. or mere bungling on the part of the District and its lawyers. If the district court determines that the former is the case, it shall impose a sanction sufficiently severe to deter any future misconduct."

In addition to problems with the amount of TVI services, there were issues about assistive technology (AT). "Because the IEP didn't specify which AT devices were being offered, M.N. had no way of confirming whether they were actually being provided to M.C. The District's failure to specify the AT devices that were provided to M.C. thus infringed M.N.'s opportunity to participate in the IEP process and denied M.C. a FAPE."

"The IDEA requires a school district to respond to a parent's due process complaint within 10 days. ... The District failed to do this and plaintiffs argue that this violated the IDEA. To be clear, the District didn't just miss a deadline: It failed to ever respond to the complaint. The district court found that the failure to respond didn't infringe M.N.'s opportunity to participate in the IEP formulation process and, therefore, wasn't a denial of a FAPE. But this misses the mark. The District's failure to respond may not have denied plaintiffs a FAPE but it still violated the IDEA and due process."

"Like an answer to a complaint, a response serves an important dual purpose: It gives notice of the issues in dispute and binds the answering party to a position. [Citations omitted.] Failure to file a response puts the opposing party at a serious disadvantage in preparing for the hearing, as it must guess what defenses the opposing party will raise."

"When a school district fails to file a timely response, the ALJ must not go forward with the hearing. Rather, it must order a response and shift the cost of the delay to the school district, regardless of who is ultimately the prevailing party. We remand for a determination of the prejudice M.N. suffered as a result of the District's failure to respond and the award of appropriate

compensation therefor." The key language, the essence of *Antelope Valley* and use of the word "potential" is below.

The Ninth Circuit emphasized that "To meet its substantive obligation under the IDEA, a school must offer an IEP reasonably calculated to enable a child to make progress appropriate in light of the child's circumstances. In other words, the school must implement an IEP that is reasonably calculated to remediate and, if appropriate, accommodate the child's disabilities so that the child can make progress in the general education curriculum, taking into account the progress of his non-disabled peers, and the child's potential. We remand so the district court can consider plaintiffs' claims in light of this new guidance from the Supreme Court."

"These procedural violations deprived M.N. of her right to participate in the IEP process and made it impossible for her to enforce the IEP and evaluate whether the services M.C. received were adequate. At the very least, plaintiffs are entitled to have the District draft a proper IEP and receive compensatory education to place M.C. in the same position he would have occupied but for the school district's violations of IDEA. [Citations omitted.] We remand the case to the district court for proceedings consistent with this opinion."

(**Wrightslaw Note:** Antelope Valley filed a Petition for a "Panel rehearing or rehearing *en banc*" that was denied. On August 28, 2017, the school district filed a notice of filing a Petition for Certiorari with SCOTUS. On December 11, 2017, SCOTUS denied the Petition for Certiorari and the case was transferred back to the U.S. District Court. On March 23, 2018, the parties filed a Joint Notice of Settlement so this case is now settled. Per a telephone call with parent attorney Christian Knox, the terms of the settlement are confidential.)

(Parent's Attorney – Christian M. Knox // School's Attorney – David R. Mishook)

Outcome: Parents prevailed.

Avila v. Spokane Sch. Dist.

9th Cir.

852 F.3d 936

Circuit Judge Christen

3/30/2017 – Washington

This is an Independent Educational Evaluation (IEE), Statute of Limitations (SOL), "knew or should have known" case in which the ALJ dismissed the parent's case. Their subsequent appeal to the U.S. District Court was also dismissed.

On appeal, the Ninth Circuit explained that in October 2006, when G.A. "was five, the Avilas asked the District to evaluate him for special education services based on behavior issues. One of the reasons for this request was a preschool teacher's concern that G.A. might be showing slight signs of autism. In December 2006, a school psychologist evaluated G.A. and concluded that although he displayed some behaviors of concern, G.A.'s behavior was not severe enough to qualify for special education services under the IDEA."

The parents did not appeal that decision by requesting a due process hearing.

One year later, in October 2007, the parents again "requested that the District reevaluate G.A.'s eligibility for special education services. A school psychologist concluded in a reevaluation dated April 14, 2008 that G.A. was eligible for special educational services under the category of autism." An "IEP was not agreed upon until February 2009." Almost a year later, "G.A. then began attending ADAPT, a specialized program in the District for students with autism."

Another year later, "the District reevaluated G.A., assessing his behavior, speech and language, occupational therapy needs, and academic achievements, including reading, writing, and mathematics. The District then drafted another IEP.

The Avilas did not agree with the reevaluation's findings and did not sign it. Instead, they requested an Independent Educational Evaluation (IEE) at the District's expense. [Citation omitted.] The District denied this request" and, per statute, initiated a due process hearing against the parents seeking a determination that their own evaluation was sufficient.

Separately, the parents filed a request for a due process hearing, raising nine procedural issues and two substantive issues. Per the U.S. District Court Opinion, by agreement of the parties, both cases were consolidated with the same ALJ.

"Ultimately, the ALJ ruled that the District's reevaluation was appropriate and that the Avilas were not entitled to an IEE at the District's expense ... [and] ruled in favor of the District on all other claims."

"The [parent's] substantive claims alleged that the District denied G.A. a free appropriate public education (FAPE) by failing to identify him as a child with a disability in 2006, and that the District failed to assess his suspected disability in 2006 and 2007. The ALJ concluded that no statutory exceptions applied and held that the Avilas' claims were time-barred." The parents due process complaint was "filed on April 26, 2010 and any complaint by Parents regarding the District actions or inactions occurring prior to April 26, 2008 are barred by the statute of limitations."

The U.S. District Court affirmed the ruling in favor of the school district. The parents appealed the IEE ruling and the ruling on their eleven claims to the Ninth Circuit.

The Ninth Circuit explained that "Congress did not intend the IDEA's statute of limitations to be governed by a strict occurrence rule. Both §1415(b)(6)(B) and §1415(f)(3)(C) include language pegging the limitations period to the date on which the parent or agency knew or should have known about the alleged action that forms the basis of the complaint, not the date on which the action occurred."

"The text and purpose of the IDEA, the DOE's interpretation of the Act, and the legislative history of the 2004 amendments all lead us to the same conclusion. We hold the IDEA's statute of limitations requires courts to apply the discovery rule without limiting redressability to the two-year period that precedes the date when 'the parent or agency knew or should have known about the alleged action that forms the basis of the complaint.'" [Citation omitted.]

"Having concluded that the IDEA's statute of limitations is triggered when the parent or agency knew or should have known about the alleged action that forms the basis of the complaint, we turn to the Avilas' claims. In dismissing the Avilas' complaint, the district court cited the correct standard from § 1415(f)(3)(C), but concluded, 'Parents' due process complaint was made April 26, 2010. Accordingly, unless an exception is shown, the Court finds any alleged misconduct prior to April 26, 2008, was not timely raised by Parents.' In other words, apart from considering the two express exceptions to the IDEA's statute of limitations, the district court barred the Avilas' claims arising before April 26, 2008 based on when the actions complained of occurred, rather than applying the discovery rule."

The Court cited other Court of Appeals cases where parents filed within two years of the date they realized that an evaluation or determination, made several years earlier, was in error. It was not the date of the school's erroneous determination regarding the eligibility classification, placement, or other issue, but the date the parent knew or should have known that the determination was erroneous.

Other courts have also held that the 'knew or had reason to know date' stems from when parents knew or had reason to know about an alleged denial of a free appropriate public education under the IDEA, not necessarily when the parents became

aware that the district acted or failed to act. This happens "where the issue is one that requires specialized expertise a parent cannot be expected to have . . ." Citing another case, parents should not be blamed for "not being experts about learning disabilities."

"Because the district court barred the Avilas' pre-April 2008 claims based on when the District's actions occurred, we remand to the district court to make findings and address the statute of limitations under the standard we adopt here, namely when the Avilas knew or should have known about the alleged actions that form the basis of the complaint."

(Parent's Attorney – Mark A. Silver // School's Attorney – Gregory Lee Stevens)

Outcome: District court reversed, case remanded. Parents prevailed.

Irvine Sch. Dist. v. K.G.
9th Cir.
853 F.3d 1087
Circuit Judge O'Scannlain
4/13/2017 – California

This convoluted case about attorneys' fees began in 2007. After a partial success, the child's attorney became ill and allowed the timeline to petition for attorneys' fees pass. The child graduated and a petition for attorney's fees was then filed by new counsel. The Ninth Circuit allowed the attorneys' fee issue to be re-opened but limited the award because the child had graduated. The Court remanded the case back to the district court to re-evaluate the attorney fee award.

The Circuit Court staff provided a "Summary" at the beginning of the decision published in Google. This Summary is not part of the ruling but is an aid to understand the ruling. Portions of the Summary are below:

"On remand from a ruling that student K.G.'s school district was the agency responsible for K.G.'s free appropriate public education, K.G. moved for statutory attorneys' fees. The district court denied the motion on the ground that K.G. was not a prevailing party but subsequently granted relief from judgment … and awarded fees."

"The [Ninth Circuit] panel held that the district court did not abuse its discretion in granting relief under Rule 60(b)(1) on the ground of excusable neglect."

"The panel held that K.G. was a prevailing party entitled to attorneys' fees because K.G. achieved the benefit sought, a decision as to which agency was responsible to provide a free appropriate public education. The panel rejected the argument that K.G. could not have benefitted from the litigation because K.G. graduated with a high school diploma months before the district court decided the case. The panel held that K.G.'s victory was not trivial or merely technical."

"The panel held, however, that it was not clear whether the amount of attorneys' fees awarded was reasonable because much of counsel's work took place after K.G.'s graduation. The panel vacated the fee award and remanded for the district court to determine whether the hours billed following K.G.'s graduation were truly the result of advocacy reasonably calculated to advance K.G.'s interests." [End of Summary.]

Two issues that may have influenced the U.S. District Court and Ninth Circuit decisions are:

"Litigation could have ceased with the decision of the ALJ. Instead, it was the School District that kept the meter running when it filed a complaint in district court."

"Once a student receives all the statutory benefits guaranteed by IDEA and no longer faces even a nominal risk that those benefits might be taken away, only exceptional circumstances can justify an ever-lengthening billing invoice. A finding that

K.G. might end up liable for bills already paid, or the possibility that his diploma might be retroactively revoked, for instance, would certainly explain the need for hundreds of hours of advocacy after his graduation in 2010. But IDEA is not 'a relief Act for lawyers.'"

"We affirm the district court's grant of relief from judgment, but we vacate the fee award. On remand, the district court shall determine whether the hours billed following K.G.'s graduation were truly the result of advocacy reasonably calculated to advance K.G.'s interests as opposed to those of K.G.'s lawyers, and the district court shall adjust the fee award accordingly with appropriate explanation."

(Parent's Attorney – Marcy J.K. Tiffany // School's Attorney – S. Daniel Harbottle)

Outcome: Parent partially prevailed as some attorneys' fees will be recovered.

R.B. v. NYC DOE
2nd Cir.
4/27/2017 - New York

In this tuition reimbursement and evaluation case, the parents were dissatisfied with the public school's IEPs and evaluation procedure. They "enrolled D.B. in a private school that specializes in educating children with autism." They requested a due process hearing to secure tuition reimbursement. The IHO ruled in their favor.

The school appealed the IHO decision to an SRO who reversed. Parents then appealed to the U.S.District Court, lost again, and appealed to the Second Circuit.

The Second Circuit explained that, after a six day hearing, "the IHO found that IEPs for both school years were insufficient because (1) the recommended vocational and transition services were deficient; (2) the Department did not give the Parents the requisite written notice for the 2013-2014 year, (3) the long-term and short-term goals specified in the IEPs were insufficiently measurable, (4) the IEPs were impermissibly predetermined, (5) the recommended classroom student to educator ratio would not allow D.B. to progress in social interactions, (6) the teaching methodology in such classrooms would be ineffective for D.B., and (7) the recommended school sites were ill-equipped to execute the IEPs' requirements."

"The IHO found that the Parents cooperated with the Department throughout the IEP development process and that the chosen private school was suitable. Therefore, the IHO concluded that the Department was obligated to reimburse D.B.'s tuition for the 2013-2014 and 2014-2015 school years."

"The Department appealed the IHO's ruling to a State Review Officer (SRO). On May 4, 2015, the SRO determined that the IEPs were sufficient and offered D.B. a FAPE."

"The SRO concluded, inter alia, that (1) the IEPs offered appropriate postsecondary goals and transition services, (2) neither IEP was predetermined, (3) omitting written notice to the parents and failing to assess D.B.'s vocational skills were mere procedural violations that did not deny D.B. a FAPE, (4) the IEPs' short and long term goals were adequate, (5) the proposed classroom student to educator ratio was reasonable, and (6) the Department did not need to specify a particular teaching methodology ahead of time."

"Therefore, the SRO concluded that the Department had offered D.B. a FAPE for the 2013-2014 and 2014-2015 school years and thus no tuition reimbursement was required."

"On appeal, the Parents principally argue that the Department was required ... to assess D.B. in person and its failure to do so undermined the development of IEPs."

"The Department explained in the state administrative proceeding that it did not conduct an in person assessment of D.B. because the Parents submitted a privately obtained substitute report and the standard vocational assessment required a higher level of reading skills than the student possessed. Moreover, the Department conducted a vocational interview with the Parents and consulted with D.B.'s private school teachers about his progress, goals, and preferred learning environment. It also invited D.B. to attend meetings in which postsecondary goals and transitions services were discussed, but the Parents declined to bring him because they felt that he could not sit through the meetings."

Citing a prior Second Circuit case in 2015, the Court also added in a footnote that "The Parents previously (but unsuccessfully) have sought reimbursement every year since 2009."

"Even assuming arguendo that the failure to assess D.B. in person was a procedural violation, we conclude that the Parents have not shown an impediment to D.B.'s right to a FAPE, a significant impediment to their opportunity to participate in the decision-making process, or a deprivation of educational benefits. Therefore, we affirm the SRO's — and the district court's — decision that the Parents are not entitled to reimbursement of D.B.'s private school tuition."

(Parent's Attorney – Gary S. Mayerson // School's Attorney – Julie Steiner)

Outcome: School prevailed.

Brittany O. v. Bentonville Sch. Dist.
8th Cir.
4/27/2017 - Arkansas

In this attorneys' fee statute of limitations (SOL) case, the parents prevailed at a special education due process hearing. The school district did not appeal the case within the 90-day statute of limitations to appeal. After 90 days passed, the parent's attorney filed a petition for attorneys' fees in the U.S. District Court.

Having failed to file for attorneys' fees within 90 days, the U.S. District Court dismissed the case explaining that the attorney filed after the SOL had passed to file for attorneys' fees. On appeal, the Eighth Circuit addressed whether the SOL for attorneys' fees begins to run from the date of the due process hearing decision or after the timeline for the school to appeal the adverse ruling.

The Eighth Circuit explained that IDEA "contains no limitations period for this type of claim, so the district court found that the most analogous state statute of limitations was an Arkansas statute providing that any party aggrieved by the findings and final decision of an officer in an administrative hearing shall have 90 days from the date of the hearing officer's decision to bring a civil action in a court of competent jurisdiction pursuant to the IDEA."

"Like the Fifth and Seventh Circuits, we conclude that whatever limitations period applies to a prevailing party's court action to recover IDEA attorneys' fees, it did not begin to run until the 90-day period had expired for an aggrieved party to challenge the IDEA administrative decision by filing a complaint in court. Upon expiration of this period, an administrative decision becomes final, and the parties know who is the prevailing party."

"Thereafter, the parties have an opportunity to agree on the matter of attorneys' fees, and if no agreement is reached, the prevailing party may bring an action in court, within the applicable limitations period, seeking attorneys' fees under the IDEA."

"Here, the 90-day period for the aggrieved party—the District—to challenge the November 25 hearing officer's decision ended on Sunday, February 23, 2014; therefore Parent's March 5, 2014 IDEA attorneys'-fees complaint was timely filed, even if the applicable limitations period was 90 days."

(Parent's Attorney – Theresa L. Caldwell // School's Attorney – Marshall S. Ney)

Outcome: U.S. District Court reversed, parent's right to attorneys' fees affirmed. Parent prevailed.

J.C. v. Katonah-Lewisboro Sch. Dist.
2nd Cir.
5/9/2017 - New York

This is a tuition reimbursement case about the deference owed to the IHO contrasted with the deference owed to the SRO in a Two-Tier State. The parents prevailed before the IHO at the Due Process Hearing. On school's appeal, the SRO reversed and parents appealed to the U.S. District Court. The Second Circuit reversed the SRO and reinstated the IHO's decision.

"T.C., now 14, suffers from multiple disabilities affecting his attention span, ability to learn, and motor skills. He attended classes at the School District from kindergarten through third grade, then transferred to a private school called the Prospect School for fourth grade through sixth."

"T.C.'s parents now seek reimbursement for tuition they paid to the Prospect School during T.C.'s fifth and sixth grades. For T.C.'s parents to prevail, they must show that: 1) the School District failed to provide T.C. with a free and appropriate public education; 2) they placed T.C. in an appropriate private school; and 3) the equities favor reimbursement."

"As is required, T.C.'s parents first sought reimbursement through New York state's administrative process before filing suit in federal court. The Initial Hearing Officer (IHO) found that the parents were entitled to reimbursement; but a State Review Officer (SRO), functioning as a second level of administrative review, reversed that decision. Courts generally owe deference to the decision of an SRO, but that deference only extends insofar as the SRO decision is well-reasoned and persuasive."

"The SRO was not required to automatically accept the neuropsychologists' recommendations as to class size, but he was required to consider the recommendations and, if he rejected them, to convincingly explain why." The SRO failed to explain why he rejected the recommendation of the neuropsychologist.

"The SRO also fails to acknowledge that the educational system tends to focus on the number of teachers in a classroom rather than the number of adults, presumably because a qualified special education teacher may be more effective than a teaching aide or assistant. Second, the SRO dismissed the neuropsychologists' recommendations on the ground that T.C.'s distraction issues could be mitigated enough so that T.C. could learn in a larger classroom. None of the evidence he relies on for that point, however, suggests that T.C.'s distraction problems could be resolved without an 8:1:1 classroom."

"We therefore agree with the district court that the SRO's ruling that the School District provided T.C. with a free and appropriate public education is entitled to diminished deference. We instead defer to the decision of the IHO, and we agree that the School District's 12:1:2 classroom would not have provided T.C. with a free and appropriate public education."

(Parent's Attorney – Lawrence D. Weinberg // School's Attorney – James P. Drohan)

Outcome: Judgment of the U.S. District Court affirmed. Parents prevailed.

D.B. v. Ithaca City Sch. Dist.
2nd Cir.

5/23/2017 - New York

In this tuition reimbursement case, Ithaca City developed the IEP based on their own and private evaluations. "Relying on the totality of these evaluations, the CSE concluded that L.B.'s education program should be provided at her home school, rather than at the residential private school recommended by D.B. and her consultant."

The SRO and the U.S. District Court ruled in favor of the school district and denied reimbursement.

On appeal to the Second Circuit, that Court discussed the "three-pronged *Burlington/Carter* test to determine eligibility for reimbursement, which looks to (1) whether the school district's proposed plan will provide the child with a FAPE; (2) whether the parents' private placement is appropriate to the child's needs; and (3) a consideration of the equities."

The parent attacked the procedural adequacy of the evaluations and the court found that any procedural testing violations did not deprive child of FAPE.

The Court found that "the IEP's recommendations align comfortably with those proffered by D.B.'s own consultant, who was concededly familiar with [Non-Verbal Learning Disability] NVLDs."

"In sum, because the record shows that L.B.'s 2012-13 IEP identified and responded to the child's learning disability, we cannot deem it substantively inadequate. [Citation omitted.] ('Whether an IEP adequately addresses a disabled student's behaviors and whether strategies for dealing with those behaviors are appropriate are precisely the type of issues upon which the IDEA requires deference to the expertise of administrative officers.'). Insofar as D.B. argues that the School District would have been unable to carry out the IEP, that contention is purely speculative and thus barred by precedent." [Citation omitted.] ('Challenges to a school district's proposed placement school must be evaluated prospectively *i.e.*, at the time of the parents' placement decision and cannot be based on mere speculation.')"

(Parent's Attorney – Edward E. Kopko // School's Attorney – Kate I. Reid)

Outcome: SRO and the U.S. District Court rulings denying tuition reimbursement affirmed. School prevailed.

D.L. v. Clear Creek Indep. Sch. Dist.

5th Cir.

6/2/2017, revised 7/31/2017 - Texas

In this eligibility and "pleading and practice" case, the child had been "diagnosed with various physical and mental ailments. Pertinently, D.L. has at one point or another been found to suffer from pervasive developmental disorder not otherwise specified, depression, attention deficit/hyperactivity disorder, and anxiety."

In May 2011, the "ARDC determined that Devon met the criteria for the IDEA disability categories of emotional disturbance and other health impairment." The following year, in April 2012, during his sophomore year, special education services were discontinued because he was no longer eligible pursuant to "teacher commendations regarding his behavior in class and toward peers, his academic performance, his lack of absences, and his assessment that his anxiety and depression were under control." D.L.'s father disagreed and requested an IEE which was completed in March 2013, almost a year after his request.

"On April 15, 2013, the ARDC met to review the IEE. The findings and recommendations from the IEE report were discussed in detail at the meeting. Devon's father expressed agreement with the IEE school recommendations. He explained that he was satisfied with the year but that Devon's performance varies by teacher and would like Devon to have a 'net' to fall back on, should support be needed in the future."

"The District acknowledged that the independent evaluator found D.L. disabled under the emotional disturbance category. But it noted that in addition to being disabled, D.L. must have an educational need to receive special education services. Based on D.L.'s experience junior year, alongside his two prior evaluations, the District decided D.L. had no such need. It further found that D.L.'s father's

concerns about possible future deterioration could be addressed through communication between school and home, a team that would monitor D.L.'s progress, and D.L.'s taking advantage of general services."

"D.L. maintained his progress during the first semester of his senior year, albeit with extensive one-off accommodations in response to requests by his father. D.L.'s father repeatedly sent emails to teachers recounting D.L.'s misbehavior at home, his reactions to recent diagnoses, his feeling overwhelmed by mounting work, and his desire to not continue in school. D.L.'s teachers were responsive to these concerns, making accommodations as necessary. The teachers' observations of D.L. stood in stark contrast to the father's reporting. They stated that he was doing great in class and that his peers looked to him for help."

In March 2014, the latter part of his senior year, the "school counselor issued a notice that Devon was in danger of not graduating due to failing grades and excessive absences. The school counselor indicated on the notice that she had attempted to meet with Devon but that he had not been attending school."

In April 2014, D.L.'s father requested a special education due process hearing and "specifically challenged the April 2013 finding that Devon did not qualify for special education services . . ." In the prehearing Order pursuant to a prehearing conference, "the hearing officer identified the pending issues as whether: (1) CCISD failed to meet its IDEA Child Find obligations by failing to identify all of Devon's disabilities in April 2013; and (2) CCISD wrongly denied Devon's eligibility for special education services and a FAPE. On the first issue, the hearing officer explained that the Child Find argument was clarified with the parties at a pre-hearing conference and determined to relate only to CCISD's April 2013 denial of special education services." The due process complaint did not allege "that the District violated the IDEA's Child Find provision by not identifying him as disabled after April 2013" and the child's possible ongoing eligibility in the last half of his senior year was not an issue pursuant to the prehearing conference and subsequent order.

The father lost at the due process hearing, appealed to the U.S. District Court, lost again, and appealed to the Court of Appeals which affirmed the prior dismissals. The Fifth Circuit noted that the school district "expressly took account of the evaluator's [IEE] report ... [but the] District chose not to adopt its recommendations ..." The Court addressed the father's fear of the future for his son "stating that fear alone … cannot form the basis for insisting that the district provide any sort of preventative special education services and noting that the child must demonstrate a present need for special education services." "In April 2013, D.L. was excelling academically and was commended by his teachers for his comportment."

"D.L.'s failure to allege in his administrative complaint that the District violated the IDEA's Child Find provision by not identifying him as disabled after April 2013 forfeits that issue. And because D.L. does not show he needed special education services in April 2013, the District was not required to provide such services."

(**Wrightslaw Note**: Some facts and quotes provided above came from the August 16, 2016 U.S. District Court decision. The July 31, 2017 amendment issued by the Fifth Circuit corrected a citation to one of the cases referenced in the Opinion.)

(**Wrightslaw Note:** The parent petitioned SCOTUS for Certiorari which was denied on April 2, 2018.) (Parent's Attorney – Mark S. Whitburn // School's Attorney – Amy Joyce Cumings Tucker)

Outcome: School prevailed.

C.E. v. Chappaqua Cent. Sch. Dist. + NYDOE

2nd Cir.

6/14/2017 – New York

In this tuition reimbursement case, the IHO ruled against the parents. On appeal, that decision was upheld by the SRO and then by the district court.

On appeal, the parents alleged that: "the IHO's decision should not be afforded deference because he was (1) biased because he had previously been a school superintendent and (2) incompetent because (a) he was not an attorney and (b) he fell asleep during portions of the hearing."

The school district alleged that the parents "failed to comply with regulations governing the font size and page limitations of submissions to SROs" and thus the parents had not "exhausted all administrative remedies, as required by the IDEA, before seeking judicial relief."

"The SRO did not dismiss the appeal on that basis but instead rendered a final decision on the merits of the Parents' claims. We therefore agree with the district court that the Parents exhausted all administrative remedies."

The Second Circuit noted the HO was not biased and "was also competent to preside over the hearing although not an attorney. The New York regulations grandfathered him status as an IHO even though he was not a lawyer ... Further, the IHO also brought decades of experience as a hearing officer to the bench."

"With regard to the Parents' assertion that the IHO was sleeping during portions of the hearing, the IHO provided an explanation for why the Parents might mistakenly think that, and our review of the portions of the record cited by the Parents confirms the district court's conclusion that the IHO was instead awake and attentive. The IHO spoke frequently, often asking questions of witnesses, ruling on objections, and addressing the admission of evidence."

"The Parents' final challenge—and their only substantive one—is to the decisions of the IHO, SRO, and district court with respect to the School District's 2011 Behavior Intervention Plan (BIP). According to the School District's expert, a BIP seeks to 'prevent the reoccurrence of behavior, to respond or manage behavior when it does occur,' and to teach appropriate alternative or replacement skills."

An FBA "is a process in which educators seek to 'determine the functions that a behavior is serving for' a student, 'with the intent of ... reinforcing or maintaining consequences around the behavior.'"

"Although the Parents frame their arguments as an attack on the School District's capacity to implement or update the 2011 BIP if needed, we conclude that their argument is best construed as a claim that the School District would not have followed through on its commitment to implement and update the BIP, not that it lacked the services required to do so."

"A School District official testified that the District was ready to update the BIP if needed, and that testimony is supported by documentary evidence. This is not a situation where a school district plainly lacks the ability to offer the services it says it will offer…The 2011 BIP was regarded as appropriate by one of the Parents' expert witnesses, Dr. Tarnell, as long as the BIP was implemented properly."

The Second Circuit upheld the findings of the IHO, the SRO, and the U.S. District Court.

(Parent's Attorney - Peter D. Hoffman // School's Attorney – Mark C. Rushfield)

Outcome: School prevailed. U.S. District Court denied tuition reimbursement.

I.T. v. Hawaii DOE

9th Cir.

6/21/2017 – Hawaii

In this appeal of an attorneys' fee award case, the U.S. District Court reduced fees "for limited success" and reduced counsel's requested hourly rate to $300. We have jurisdiction ... [and] review for an abuse of discretion." [Citation omitted.]

"In Individuals with Disabilities Education Act (IDEA) cases, district courts may reduce attorney's fees based on the plaintiff's degree of success in the litigation. [Citation omitted.] I.T.'s success in this case was clearly limited, given that he prevailed on only one narrow issue—the lack of speech-language services in two individualized education plans—and obtained only thirteen percent of the relief he requested. [Citation omitted.] A reduced fee award is appropriate if the relief, however significant, is limited in comparison to the scope of the litigation as a whole. The district court thoroughly explained its reductions, devoting several pages to the limited success analysis. [Citation omitted.] When the district court makes its award, it must explain how it came up with the amount. The explanation need not be elaborate, but it must be comprehensible. Accordingly, the district court did not abuse its discretion in reducing the fee motions by twenty percent for limited success."

"The district court also did not abuse its discretion by reducing counsel's requested hourly rate to $300. The IDEA requires that any fee award be based on rates prevailing in the community in which the action or proceeding arose for the kind and quality of services furnished. [Citation omitted.] I.T.'s request for a $400 rate here is largely predicated on a 2013 decision by the Hawaii Supreme Court ... [which] did not establish the prevailing rate in the community for similar work performed by attorneys of comparable skill, experience, and reputation. [Citation omitted.] Moreover, we recently affirmed an hourly rate of

$285 for a similar IDEA case in Hawaii. [Citation omitted.] Accordingly, the district court did not abuse its discretion in finding that an hourly rate of $300 was consistent with prevailing rates in the community."

In Hawaii, the "Local Education Agency" (LEA) is also, for practical purposes, also the State Education Agency (SEA), thus the Hawaii Department of Education is the defendant.

(**Wrightslaw Note**: A subsequent Petition for Certiorari to SCOTUS was denied.)

(Attorney information not provided by Google.)

Outcome: U.S. District Court reduction upheld. Hawaii prevailed.

DL v. DCPS

DC Cir.

860 F.3d 713

Circuit Judge Tatel

6/23/2017 - Washington, DC

This "child find" class action case began in 2005 when "the parents of six children, ages three to six, sued the District, alleging a 'pervasive and systemic' breakdown in the school system's Child Find program. According to the complaint, the District was failing to identify large numbers of disabled children and delivering inadequate and delayed services to many others. These deficiencies, the parents argued, were depriving 'hundreds' of preschoolers of their right to a FAPE." The U.S. District Court "found the District liable for violating its Child Find obligations and failing to ensure a smooth and effective transition for toddlers entering preschool."

The case went through several procedural hurdles related to the definition of a "class" and, eventually, "After considering testimony from seventeen witnesses and reviewing hundreds of exhibits, the district court issued a 130-page opinion finding the District liable for violating IDEA ... and the District had yet to attain a period of sustained compliance."

DCPS asserted that the case should be dismissed. "As the District sees it, the 'proper role' of IDEA's judicial enforcement provision is individualized rather than systemic relief."

The DC Circuit Court held that "The District's argument would eviscerate the very purpose of IDEA. When Congress enacted the legislation that became IDEA, it was responding to the 'pervasive and tragic' failure to serve all children with disabilities, *Endrew F.*, 137 S. Ct. at 999, which is why it imposed on states accepting IDEA funding an obligation to identify, locate, and evaluate all preschoolers with disabilities. Yet the District, which has enthusiastically accepted millions of dollars in IDEA funding, now proposes to shift that burden back to the parents."

"In the District's view, it would be up to each and every parent, many of whom are poor, homeless, and perhaps disabled themselves, to somehow determine whether their children are eligible for special education services and then to retain counsel to sue the District to obtain the services to which they are entitled. Given the purpose of IDEA, we cannot imagine a more preposterous argument. And given the district court's finding that the District has failed, year after year, to comply with IDEA's Child Find requirement, we have no doubt that the statute's remedial provision - authorizing courts to grant such relief as they determine is appropriate, and implicating broad discretion and equitable considerations, - vests the court with all the authority it needs to remedy those violations through injunctive relief."

In closing, the DC Court of Appeals said "Having considered each of the District's challenges, we are convinced that the district court made no mistake. So long as the District of Columbia accepts federal funding, it is bound to its pledge to find, evaluate, and serve all children with disabilities. The district court neither erred nor abused its discretion in holding the District to its word. We affirm in all respects."

(Parent's Attorney – Todd A. Gluckman // School's Attorney – Lucy E. Pittman // COPAA Amicus Attorney – Selene Almazan-Altobelli)

Outcome: The DC Circuit Court of Appeals upheld the U.S. District Court and the class of parents prevailed.

C.G. v. Waller Indep. Sch. Dist.
5th Cir.
Circuit Judge Weiner
6/29/2017 - Texas

In this tuition reimbursement case, the child has autism and pervasive developmental delays. For two years, pursuant to the public school's IEP, the child received instruction in the special education classroom. "Dissatisfied with C.G.'s progress, her parents rejected WISD's proposed IEP for the 2013-14 school year and proposed extended school year services for the 2013 summer. They enrolled C.G. in a private school, retained certified special education teachers and specialists, and assembled private speech therapy sessions."

The parents requested a due process hearing seeking reimbursement for the private placement. The HO held that "WISD had provided C.G. a FAPE because her IEPs were appropriate and the least restrictive environment for her educational benefit."

"The parents appealed the TEA's decision to the district court and added a claim of discrimination under § 504 of the Rehabilitation Act. They moved for judgment on the administrative record, seeking reimbursement for C.G.'s private placement and injunctive relief under § 504 for discrimination. WISD moved for summary judgment on all claims. The district court granted WISD's motion for summary judgment and denied the parents' motion for judgment on the administrative record."

The Fifth Circuit explained that "Our court has set forth four factors for determining if an IEP is reasonably calculated: (1) the program is individualized on the basis of student's assessment and performance; (2) the program is administered in the least restrictive environment; (3) the services are provided in a coordinated and collaborative manner by the key stakeholders; and (4) positive academic and non-academic benefits are demonstrated."

"These factors are ... intended to guide a district court in the fact-intensive inquiry of evaluating whether an IEP provided an educational benefit, and no factor is afforded more or less weight than the others."

The U.S. District Court decision was issued before SCOTUS issued its ruling in *Endrew F.*. The Fifth Circuit had to determine if that earlier ruling conflicted with *Endrew F.*. They concluded that it did not, explaining "Although the district court did not articulate the standard set forth in *Endrew F.* verbatim, its analysis of C.G.'s IEP is fully consistent with that standard and leaves no doubt that the court was convinced that C.G.'s IEP was appropriately ambitious in light of her circumstances."

With regard to the Section 504 claim, "C.G.'s parents claim that by placing every disabled student, including C.G., into the highly restrictive zoned classroom, WISD discriminated against C.G." The Fifth Circuit disagreed and explained that "The district court did not err in concluding that the § 504 claim should be dismissed because it was not independent of C.G.'s IDEA claim."

(Parent's Attorney – Mark S. Whitburn // School's Attorney – Holly Gene McIntush)

Outcome: the U.S. District Court denial of tuition reimbursement upheld. School district prevailed.

Special School District 1 v. R.M.M.
8th Cir.

861 F.3d 769

Circuit Judge Shepherd

6/29/2017 - Minnesota

This case is about the rights of a child with special education needs who attends a private school. The legal issue relates to Minnesota law, not federal law.

While R.M.M. was enrolled in a private school, her parents filed a due process complaint against their local school district.

The Eighth Circuit explained that "This case is about the provision of special education services to a young child attending a nonpublic school. Federal law grants this child neither an individual right to a free appropriate public education nor the right to dispute the provision of special education services in a due process hearing. The question before us is whether Minnesota state law grants either of these rights."

The Eighth Circuit explained that "On the issue of R.M.M.'s right to a FAPE, the district court first analyzed federal law. The court found that federal law did not grant the right to a FAPE to a private school student but did permit states to grant rights beyond the minimum requirements set out by federal law. Turning to Minnesota state law, the court held that Minnesota granted private school students the right to a FAPE. On the issue of a due process hearing, the court ruled in favor of R.M.M. and held that private school students in Minnesota are entitled to a due process hearing to dispute whether they have received a FAPE. MPS now appeals."

The Court of Appeals noted that "all children with disabilities attending public school have possessed a substantive right to a FAPE since the enactment of IDEA. But the rights afforded by IDEA to a child with disabilities attending private school have changed over time."

"Prior to 1997, students with disabilities attending private schools possessed an individual right to special education and related services ... Then, in 1997, Congress amended IDEA. 'These amendments substantially limited the rights of disabled children enrolled by their parents in a private school. [Citation omitted.] No longer do private school students have an individual right to special education and related services based on their needs. See 34 C.F.R. § 300.137(a) No parentally-placed private school child with a disability has an individual right to receive some or all of the special education and related services that the child would receive if enrolled in a public school. Instead, private school students as a group now receive services based on proportionate-share funding."

"Minnesota has long guaranteed special education services for children with disabilities under state law ... current Minnesota state law demands that every district must provide special instruction and services ... for all children with a disability, [and] no resident of a district who is eligible for special instruction and services ... shall be denied provision of this instruction and service on a shared time basis because of attendance at a nonpublic school."

"[T]his is a case about statutory interpretation. And the plain language of Minnesota law grants both the right to a FAPE and the right to an impartial due process hearing to children with disabilities attending nonpublic schools. For the reasons discussed herein, we affirm the district court."

(Parent's Attorney – Roseann Schreifels // School's Attorney – Amy Jane Goetz)

Outcome: The District Court ruling was upheld. Parents prevailed.

R.A. v. West Contra Costa Unif. Sch. Dist.

9th Cir

6/30/2017 - California

This convoluted and difficult to follow case is about a settlement agreement and terms and conditions relating to an evaluation of the child.

The Ninth Circuit provided very few facts about the history, so it was necessary to review the U.S. District Court opinion to understand the issues.

Near the end of the terms and timeline of a settlement agreement with evaluation issues, the parents requested a due process hearing. The ALJ and the U.S. District Court ruled against the parents, finding that the public school's IEP was appropriate, that the parent did not have a right to observe the school's testing of the child, that the parents proposed placement was not the least restrictive environment (LRE) and that the school's proposed placement was not predetermined.

The Court found that "The District did not deny R.A. a FAPE by failing to complete behavior and psychoeducational assessments. The record reflects that the District did not carry out the assessments because of an impasse over the testing-room conditions R.A.'s mother required and the testing-room protocols required by Dr. April Jourdan, the District examiner. There is no legal requirement for the District to let R.A.'s mother see and hear R.A. during the behavioral and psychoeducational assessment, the condition R.A.'s mother insisted was necessary." As noted in the District Court decision, the parent proposed use of a one-way mirror.

The proposed placement issue, as described by the U.S. District Court, explained that the school's IEP team "members testified that they considered the programs being recommended by Ms. Riehle — continuation of the home-based program — and Dr. Habash [the parent] — a one-on-one program in a separate classroom on a public school campus with an ABA-trained teacher and interaction with

ABA-trained peer mentors for approximately one hour per day — were too restrictive for Student."

"He has received all his educational instruction and services through the in-home program funded by the District. In this program, he has been schooled using a program that was developed and supervised by his mother ('Mother' or 'Dr. Habash'). Plaintiffs allege that this program employed ABA techniques 100% of the time and was implemented one-on-one by a credentialed ABA-trained certified teacher chosen by Dr. Habash."

The school district offered to place the child into Anova, "a certified non-public school designed to serve students who are living with autism, ADHD-specific learning disabilities, speech and language impairments, and other disabling conditions recognized by the state of California in a setting that is primarily academic in nature."

Per the U.S. District Court "Plaintiffs contend that Anova was not the LRE because all the students at Anova are disabled, with the majority on the autism spectrum. They argue that in such an environment, Student would be deprived of contact with typically developing peers with whom he could learn to socialize."

"Here, it is difficult to see how placement at Anova constituted a more restrictive environment than the proposal of R.A.'s parents, which envisioned individualized, one-on-one instruction within the walls of a public school but without actual integration into public school classes. If anything, the evidence suggested that R.A.'s parents' proposed placement was significantly more restrictive than placement at Anova. The record therefore reflects that the District placed R.A. in the least restrictive environment available."

(Attorney information not provided by Google.)

Outcome: School prevailed.

I.Z.M. v. Rosemount-Apple
Valley Eagan Pub. Sch.
8th Cir.
863 F.3d 966
Circuit Judge Loken
7/14/2017 - Minnesota

This post-*Endrew F.* case is about the appropriateness of an educational program for a child with visual impairments.

"I.Z.M. suffers from severe vision problems [and his IEP] provided that he will use Braille for all classroom assignments and instruction and specified other supplemental aids and services to be provided." Upset with the school's failure to provide these services, the parents requested a due process hearing.

"After a four-day evidentiary hearing, a state Administrative Law Judge issued a thirty-nine-page Order and supporting Memorandum concluding that the District provided I.Z.M. a FAPE and dismissing the complaint." The parents appealed to the U.S. District Court which granted the school district's "motions for judgment on the administrative record on the IDEA claim and for summary judgment on the non-IDEA claims."

The U.S. District Court explained that there was "(1) significant evidence showed the District took steps to provide I.Z.M. accessible instructional materials in a timely manner; (2) to the extent the District may have imperfectly complied with IEP requirements, the IDEA does not require perfection; and (3) I.Z.M. received an educational benefit from the services the District provided, as reflected by his grades. To the extent the evidence showed a lack of progress on I.Z.M.'s Braille reading speed, the district court agreed with the ALJ that this was more likely due to I.Z.M.'s persistence in reading visually rather than tactually."

In footnote 3, the Eighth Circuit noted that "One IEP goal was for I.Z.M. to 'increase his average [Braille] reading rate from 80 to 95 words per minute.' Over the course of I.Z.M.'s ninth-grade year, his Braille reading speed dropped from 80 to 40 words per minute."

"On appeal, I.Z.M. argues the district court applied the wrong legal standards in upholding the ALJ's decision. First, with respect to the IEP provision requiring Braille instruction, I.Z.M. argues that the Minnesota Blind Persons' Literacy Rights and Education Act, Minn. Stat. § 125A.06, imposed on the District an absolute obligation, enforceable in an IDEA lawsuit, to provide instruction in Braille reading and writing that enables each blind student to communicate with the same level of proficiency expected of the student's peers. Second, with respect to the IEP provision requiring accessible instructional materials, I.Z.M. argues that a federal Department of Education regulation, 34 C.F.R. § 300.172, requires strict compliance that is not satisfied by a determination merely that the student made some educational progress. We reject both contentions and affirm dismissal of I.Z.M.'s IDEA claims."

With regard to the Section 504 vis á vis IDEA claims, the Court explained that "a disabled student's § 504 and ADA claims of unlawful discrimination are not precluded [barred] if they are wholly unrelated to the IEP process. [Citation omitted.] [O]n the other hand, I.Z.M.'s specific claims of unlawful discrimination all grew out of or were intertwined with allegations that the District failed to properly implement his IEP, allegations that were necessarily resolved in rejecting his IDEA claims. Putting this preclusion issue aside, the district court concluded, even if Plaintiffs' non-IDEA claims are not entirely precluded [barred] by the judgment in favor of the School District on the IDEA claim, they fail as a matter of law because Plaintiffs have not demonstrated the existence of a genuine issue of material fact regarding the School District's bad faith or gross misjudgment."

"The judgment of the district court is affirmed."

(**Wrightslaw Note**: COPAA filed an Amicus Brief on behalf of the parents.)

(Parent's Attorney – Andrea Jepsen // School's Attorney – Timothy R. Palmatier // COPAA Amicus Attorney – Judith A. Gran)

Outcome: The Court affirmed "dismissal of I.Z.M.'s IDEA [and 504] claims." School prevailed.

C.G.; R.G. v. Winslow Township Bd. Ed.
3rd Cir.
Circuit Judge Rendell
7/19/2017 – New Jersey

In this attorneys' fee case, the plaintiffs appealed the U.S. District Court's ruling that barred their attorney "from personally videotaping depositions during the course of a fee dispute" and also appealed the reduction of the attorney fee award from the requested $160,731 to $47,212.50. "The fee dispute arose out of the settlement" and IEP and accommodation plan. The settlement agreement between Parents and Winslow awarded attorney's fees, presumably of an undetermined amount, to parents.

"The [deposition] notices indicated that the depositions would be transcribed and recorded by video, but did not state that Plaintiffs' counsel intended to record the depositions himself on his laptop." In other words, unlike usual procedures, the attorney did not use a certified Court Reporter to take the deposition testimony.

In its ruling, the Court of Appeals explained that "The Magistrate Judge ruled that Plaintiffs' counsel could not personally videotape the deposition. ... In particular, an oral deposition must be conducted by an 'officer,' [citation omitted] and Plaintiffs' attorney did not qualify as an 'officer,' which is defined as either a person appointed by the court or

a person designated by the parties under Rule 29(a). Fed. R. Civ. P. 28(a)(2)."

"The District Court's 50% lodestar reduction was based on Plaintiffs' attorney's excessive billing in this case, including for entries he had previously withdrawn, and the carelessness at best with which he drafted his fee request. Cast against Plaintiffs' attorney's well-documented history of egregious conduct in fee requests in the District of New Jersey and of grossly overstating his fees, the inappropriate reaching for fees in this case shocked the conscience of the District Court."

The Court of Appeals did not permit the parent's attorney to personally videotape the depositions and affirmed the attorney fee reduction from $160,731 to $47,212.50.

(Attorney information not provided by Google.)

Outcome: School prevailed.

Dallas Indep. Sch. Dist. v. Woody
5th Cir.
865 F.3d 303
Circuit Judge Southwick
7/27/2017 - Texas

This tuition reimbursement "comparable IEP" case has an unusual factual scenario. Woody, the parent "sought reimbursement for the cost of her daughter's private-school tuition. The hearing officer found for Woody, awarding her $25,426.93. The district court affirmed but reduced the award to $11,942.50. The school district appealed. Woody did not."

The Fifth Circuit described this as a "unique factual situation." Woody's daughter, Kelsey, started high school in a Dallas private school, then moved to Los Angeles [LAUSD], initially enrolled in a private school, and then into a public school.

After evaluations of the child in May 2012, the LAUSD "IEP team met and concluded that Kelsey was eligible for services [and the] IEP designated general education, which meant a public school, as her proper instructional setting." That summer the child had a psychotic break. She was admitted to a psychiatric hospital. Her "doctors recommended a specialized learning environment" so, in September 2012, her mother moved her daughter back to Dallas, where she lived with her godparents. She was enrolled "at the private Winston School, which offered a specialized learning environment for students with learning disabilities. Kelsey's performance improved, but she continued to receive psychiatric treatment."

"Meanwhile, Woody initiated a due-process action against LAUSD to challenge its failure to offer Kelsey private-school placement. The parties settled in April 2013, and LAUSD agreed to reimburse Woody for educational costs associated with Kelsey's placement at the Winston School and for counseling services during the 2012-13 school year. LAUSD also agreed to place Kelsey at an appropriate non-public school for the 2013-14 school year. LAUSD's May 2013 IEP placed Kelsey at the Westview School in California, not the Winston School in Dallas."

The mother "moved back to Dallas in August 2013 and Kelsey became a resident of the Dallas School District." On September 16, 2013, the mother notified Dallas of Kelsey's new residence [and her] desire for Kelsey to receive FAPE in the form of tuition reimbursement. She provided the LAUSD IEP from May 2013 that placed Kelsey in a non-public school for her senior year and indicated that she was a student with a disability."

"Kelsey remained at the Winston School that fall. As the district court found, the record is clear that Woody believed it critical for Kelsey to remain at the Winston School and intended, from the beginning, to pursue funding for her tuition from the District."

In December 2013, the mother met with the school staff. The school district "rejected LAUSD's IEP

and planned to evaluate Kelsey and develop its own IEP. The District was aware of Kelsey's disabilities (including her diagnosis of schizophrenia) and Children Medical Center's recommendations. It was also aware that LAUSD had found her to be eligible for special-education services under IDEA. It did not offer temporary services but instead sought consent to evaluate Kelsey."

A considerable amount of time passed as records were secured, Dallas completed an FIE [Full and Individual Evaluation] and "provided it to Woody on April 8, 2014. The initial FIE found Kelsey to be IDEA-eligible. On April 16, though, the District gave Woody a revised FIE in which its psychologist concluded Kelsey was not IDEA-eligible due to her successful performance in the 'mainstream' environment at the Winston School."

After an IEE, "the ARD Committee reconvened on May 22. It determined that Kelsey was IDEA-eligible and developed an IEP for Kelsey to be implemented at a District high school from April 2014 to April 2015. Kelsey was to graduate in May 2014, though."

(**Wrightslaw Note**: In Texas, the ARD / Admission, Review, and Dismissal Committee is an IEP Committee.)

"The May 22 proposed IEP was the District's first attempt to offer FAPE. That summer, Woody's psychologist completed an IEE and provided it to the District. The District never reconvened the ARD Committee to consider the IEE, so the district court found that the District never finalized the May 2014 IEP, thereby never finalizing its offer of FAPE."

"In October 2014, Woody requested a due-process hearing. The hearing officer concluded that the District had a legal obligation to make a timely offer of FAPE available to Kelsey for the 2013-14 school year. Because it failed to do so, the hearing officer concluded that the mother was entitled to reimbursement in the amount of $25,426.93, an amount that covered the cost of sending Kelsey to the Winston School for the entire 2013-14 school year."

The school district appealed to the U.S. District Court which partially affirmed "agreeing that the District impeded Kelsey's right to FAPE for 2013-14, but it reduced the reimbursement award to $11,942.50 finding that Woody's conduct contributed in part to the imbroglio before the court."

The Fifth Circuit also provided an extensive analysis about the "comparable IEP" concept regarding children with IEPs who move and change school districts. In this scenario, "the facts of this case may expose a gap in IDEA's coverage. A school district had already determined that Kelsey was disabled under IDEA, but after moving to a new district in a new state, she still had to wait through a successive evaluation to gain entitlement to services. All along, there was uncertainty about whether there would be reimbursement."

"Kelsey, though, does not fit under either provision. First, she was weeks into her second year at the Winston School before the District was notified of a new, potentially eligible student within its boundaries. Thus, her circumstances did not trigger the District's obligations under Section 300.323(a)."

Yet "a student who already has an IEP (from anywhere) indicating a disability and therefore eligibility under IDEA and who lives in the district's jurisdiction falls within Section 300.323(a). A school district must have an IEP in place for such a student at the beginning of each school year."

In resolving the facts and legal issues, the Fifth Circuit explained that "We consider these events, though, to be a substantive failure to offer FAPE from at least April 24 until the end of the semester. The District was obligated to offer an IEP reasonably calculated to enable a child to make progress appropriate in light of the child's

circumstances. See *Endrew F.* It did not. Kelsey had completed her coursework and was scheduled to graduate in a week. Placing her in public school for her final week of school would have been nonsensical and potentially devastating."

"Thus, reimbursement may be calculated from the date the District should have provided FAPE under the Act — but not earlier. Relevant to when the District should have acted are its child-find obligations, under which it was required to identify, locate, and evaluate all children with disabilities residing in the State, such as Kelsey, including ... children with disabilities attending private schools ... 20 U.S.C. § 1412(a)(3)."

"Reimbursement should therefore be awarded from April 24, 2014, when FAPE should have been offered, until the end of the school year."

Failure to provide a "comparable IEP" in a timely manner may open the door to private school tuition reimbursement.

(**Wrightslaw Note**: The "comparable IEP" statute for a child with an IEP who moves from one school district to another is located at 20 U.S.C. § 1414(d)(2)(C) and is in *Wrightslaw: Special Education Law, 2ⁿᵈ Ed.* beginning at page 102. See the footnotes at the bottom of that page about IEPs being "similar" or "equivalent" for the child who moves.)

(**Wrightslaw Note**: COPAA filed an Amicus Brief on behalf of the parents.)

(Parent's Attorney – Roy Tress Attwood // School's Attorney – Dianna Dawn Bowen // COPAA Amicus Attorney - Selene Almazan-Altobelli)

Outcome: The Court remanded case back to the U.S. District Court to recalculate the reimbursement award. Parent prevailed.

Jefferson County Bd. Ed. v. Brian M, Darcy M

11th Cir.

8/11/2017 – Alabama

In this attorneys' fees / mootness case, the parents prevailed as the hearing officer found that "the school district had developed an inappropriate behavior intervention plan for R.M., failed to provide him with appropriate treatment, and did not treat them as equal partners in developing the IEP. The Parents also invoked the 'stay put' provision, which the state hearing officer concluded required R.M. to remain at Snow Rogers."

The HO also found that "the school system had improperly predetermined the placement ... that the school district had failed to properly implement R.M.'s behavior plan; and that the school district had violated R.M.'s right to receive educational services in the least restrictive environment."

Later, "although the Parents initially enrolled R.M. at Mount Olive for the 2014-2015 school year, they withdrew him again two days before classes started. They have not indicated to the Board that they have any intention of re-enrolling R.M. in the Jefferson County school system or any other public school."

The district court concluded that since "R.M. was no longer a student in the Jefferson County schools, its appeal and the portion of the Parent's counterclaim asking that the hearing officer's order be affirmed were moot. The district court next explained that the Parents were entitled to attorney's fees as prevailing parties under § 1415, even though any appeal from the merits of the due process ruling was moot. The district court declined to vacate the hearing officer's order. This is the Board's appeal."

"The Board asks us to reverse the district court's conclusion that the Parents are prevailing parties and its refusal to vacate the state hearing officer's order. ... The district court was correct that the Board's appeal is moot."

"The Parents' counterclaim is also moot [since] R.M. has left the Jefferson County school system and apparently has no intention to return."

"Despite the mootness of the Board's appeal and the Parents' counterclaim, the district court concluded that the Parents were prevailing parties entitled to attorney's fees under 20 U.S.C. § 1415. The Board appeals that conclusion, arguing that neither the Parents nor their son received any benefit from the due process order. We disagree with the Board and agree with the district court."

In quoting an earlier Eleventh Circuit case, when "plaintiffs clearly succeeded in obtaining relief sought before the district court and an intervening event rendered the case moot on appeal, plaintiffs are still 'prevailing parties' for the purposes of attorney's fees for the district court litigation."

"Both the Supreme Court and this Court have made clear that parents are not required to keep their student in a learning environment they believe violates the IDEA while due process proceedings are pending."

"In sum, this case is moot, the Parents and R.M. qualify as 'prevailing parties' entitled to reasonable attorney's fees, and the hearing officer's order should not be vacated."

(**Wrightslaw Note**: COPAA filed an Amicus Brief on behalf of the parents.)

(Parent's Attorney – Alice K. Nelson // School's Attorney – James R. Gallini // COPAA Amicus Attorney – Selene Almazan-Altobelli)

Outcome: Although the case is moot, parents prevailed and recovered attorneys' fees.

M.L. v. Montgomery County Bd. Ed. + Supt. Smith

4th Cir.

867 F.3d 487

Circuit Judge Agee

8/14/2017 - Maryland

In this tuition reimbursement case, the parents wanted their son to be "taught about the Torah, kosher rules, and Orthodox Jewish garments ... instructed, as part of his IEP, in *halacha* (Jewish law) and *mitzvot* ('commandments from God') ... and instruction in the *berachot*, which is [the] blessing that Orthodox Jews make before they partake in food and a blessing that they make when they finish partaking in food. ... [and] that he be able to read Hebrew."

"The Plaintiffs demand that MCPS provide this instruction to M.L. as part of his IEP."

The Fourth Circuit noted that "The facts are largely undisputed. M.L. was born in 2003 with Down Syndrome and is considered a child with a disability under the IDEA. [Citation omitted.] He and his family are members of the Orthodox Jewish faith and reside in an Orthodox Jewish community in Montgomery County, Maryland."

"The tenets of Orthodox Judaism include instruction that the Jewish Bible and Jewish law and custom govern how an Orthodox Jew dresses, eats, prays, works, what holidays are celebrated, and almost every aspect of life, including social interaction and understanding and speaking Hebrew."

"In 2009, M.L. was enrolled, at his parents' expense, in Sulam, a special education program that serves the Orthodox Jewish community. In 2012, the Plaintiffs and MCPS met to form an individualized education program (IEP) for M.L. so that he could attend classes in the public school district. After expert assessments of M.L.'s capabilities, MCPS determined that M.L. is able to learn despite his severe intellectual disability, but he needs constant repetition and consistency."

"After multiple meetings with the Plaintiffs, MCPS created an IEP for M.L. in 2013. The Plaintiffs, however, rejected the IEP because it does not provide functional instruction to prepare M.L. for life in the Orthodox Jewish community. Rather, the Plaintiffs wanted the incorporation of goals and objectives designed to teach M.L. about the laws and customs of Orthodox Judaism. MCPS rejected this proposal in turn because it was not part of the curriculum, too specific, religious, or not compatible with M.L.'s present levels. Shortly thereafter, the Plaintiffs filed a due process complaint against MCPS with the Maryland Office of Administrative Hearings, alleging violations of the IDEA and Maryland state law."

"The ALJ concluded that neither the IDEA nor Maryland law requires a public school to provide religious instruction to disabled students as part of an IEP. According to the ALJ, a FAPE primarily requires that a school provide the disabled student with access to the general curriculum. Nothing in the IDEA, corresponding State law, or enabling regulations require a state educational agency to individualize an educational program to a disabled child's religion, culture, or community enclave. Ultimately, the ALJ found the IEP proposed by MCPS provided M.L. with a FAPE under the IDEA. In view of that holding, it was not necessary for the ALJ to address any of the Establishment Clause defenses made by MCPS."

In its ruling affirming the ALJ, the "district court held that the IDEA does not require a school system to instruct disabled students in the customs and practice of Orthodox Judaism as part of a free appropriate public education (FAPE). For the reasons stated below, we affirm the judgment of the district court."

In closing, the Fourth Circuit concluded that "MCPS provided M.L. with equal access to an education, on the same basis as it provides to all other students with disabilities. It does not provide religious and cultural instruction to its students with or without disabilities and has no duty under the IDEA to administer such instruction to M.L. Thus, because the proposed IEP provided M.L. with a FAPE, it meets the requirements of the IDEA. The district court did not err in so finding and awarding summary judgment to MCPS."

(**Wrightslaw Note**: The parents unsuccessfully petitioned SCOTUS for a Writ of Certiorari.)

(Parent's Attorney - Michael Eig // School's Attorney – Jeffrey A. Krew)

Outcome: School prevailed.

M.R.; J.R. v. Ridley Sch. Dist.
3rd Cir.
868 F.3d 218
Circuit Judge Krause
8/22/2017 – Pennsylvania

This is an attorneys' fee / "stay put" case. Parents requested a due process hearing seeking tuition reimbursement for their child's private placement accusing "Ridley of 'fail[ing] to develop an appropriate IEP'" for their daughter.

"The administrative hearing officer agreed with E.R.'s parents and ... opined that Ridley's proposed IEPs 'were inadequate and therefore denied E.R. a free appropriate public education.' This decision in the parents' favor during the administrative review process equated to 'an agreement between the State and the parents' and rendered E.R.'s private-school placement her 'then-current educational placement' for purposes of the IDEA's 'stay put' provision. [Citation omitted.] Beginning at that point, therefore, Ridley was obliged to reimburse E.R.'s parents for their private-school costs."

However, the school district appealed the HO's decision to the U.S. District Court which reversed. Parents appealed to the Third Circuit, which upheld the district court.

In that instance, at what point does the school district's obligation under "stay put" to fund the private placement cease? If the school district had already partially funded the private placement pending the District Court decision, is the school district entitled to a refund?

With the parent's appeal to the Third Circuit, must the school district, under "stay put" continue to fund the private placement until a final ruling from that Court of Appeals? Although the parents lost the primary case on the merits, are they entitled to recovery of attorney's fees for the "stay put" litigation?

(**Wrightslaw Note**: The stay put statute, also known as the pendency statute, is located at 20 U.S.C. § 1415(j) and in *Wrightslaw: Special Education Law, 2nd Ed.* at page 118. See our footnotes 153 and 154 on that page for more information.)

In accord with "stay put," the parents requested reimbursement for the private placement from the date of Hearing Officer's decision through the final, adverse, determination by the Third Circuit. Ridley refused to pay the "stay put" reimbursement. The parents sued for recovery of that tuition and also for their attorney's fees in seeking the "stay put" reimbursement.

"This time, the District Court ruled in the parents' favor. [Citation omitted.] Although Ridley asserted a trio of defenses — claim preclusion, the parents' alleged failure to bring a compulsory counterclaim under Federal Rule of Civil Procedure 13(a) in their first suit, and the IDEA's ninety-day statute of limitations — the District Court rejected each of them, concluding that Ridley's reimbursement obligations began once the hearing officer issued her decision in E.R.'s parents' favor and continued through the completion of the appeals process."

"On appeal, we affirmed the District Court's decision on the reimbursement issue in full. [Citation omitted.] Ridley then petitioned the

Supreme Court for a writ of certiorari, which was denied on May 18, 2015. [Citation omitted.] Only after that denial did Ridley reimburse E.R.'s parents as the District Court had ordered in 2012."

"Having finally obtained the reimbursement they sought, E.R.'s parents filed a motion for an award of attorneys' fees under the IDEA's attorneys' fees provision, 20 U.S.C. § 1415(i)(3)(B)(i), but the District Court denied the motion, holding that reimbursement for the costs of E.R.'s temporary stay put placement was only interim relief and thus E.R.'s parents were not prevailing parties. This appeal followed."

The Court of Appeals noted that: "when a school district violates its 'stay put' obligations and parents must take action — whether by motion or by separate complaint — to obtain retrospective compensatory relief, then, for all practical purposes, the resulting proceedings are separate from any IEP or educational placement proceedings."

"[I]f a school district refuses to provide or pay for the child's then-current educational placement, the stay put provision establishes the parents' right to monetary reimbursement or, alternatively, the child's right to compensatory education, both of which are rights to backward-looking compensatory relief and require an independent merits determination."

"We hold today that such relief is merits-based and confers prevailing party status."

"For the avoidance of doubt, and given that there is no exhaustion requirement for actions seeking relief under the IDEA's stay put provision, [citation omitted] we hold that parents who obtain backward-looking compensatory relief are prevailing parties under the IDEA, whether they first pursue such relief in an administrative agency or in a court. ... [W]e conclude, contrary to the District Court's decision, that E.R.'s parents in fact

are prevailing parties under § 1415(i)(3)(B)(i) and thus are eligible for a fee award."

(Parent's Attorney – Alan L. Yatkin // School's Attorney – John Francis X. Reilly)

Outcome: Parents prevailed and recovered attorneys' fees.

Rachel H. v. Hawaii DOE
9th Cir.
868 F.3d 1085
Circuit Judge Fisher
8/29/2017 – Hawaii

"Rachel's parents argued their daughter was denied a free appropriate public education because of a purported procedural error, specifically, not identifying the anticipated school where special education services would be delivered in light of a planned move to a new school district."

"In 2012, Rachel was finishing ninth grade at a private school paid for, in part, by the Hawaii Department of Education (Department) under a settlement agreement with Rachel's parents. In May of that year, the Department held an individualized education program (IEP) meeting to determine the special education services Rachel would receive in the upcoming school year. During the meeting, Rachel's father urged the Department to continue paying for Rachel's tuition at the private school, but the Department declined."

"At the time of the May 2012 IEP meeting, all parties involved understood that the 'public school campus' offered by the Department was Kalani High School. However, neither Rachel's IEP nor the prior written notice of the proposed changes formally identified the anticipated school where Rachel's tenth grade IEP would be implemented."

"Rachel's parents did not sign the May 2012 IEP. A few months later, Rachel's father informed the

Department that the family was moving to Kailua, approximately 20 to 30 miles from Kalani High School. Consequently, according to Rachel's father, Kalani would under no circumstances be Rachel's local public high school given the distance from the school to their new home. He again demanded to enroll Rachel in private school at public expense."

"The Department did not accede to this demand. On July 30, 2012, it wrote Rachel's parents that the May 2012 IEP was not specific to Kalani High School. Instead, the IEP was based on Rachel's current strengths and needs. Accordingly, the Department asked for the family's new address in Kailua so the location where Rachel's IEP can be implemented can be determined. Until the family's move, Rachel could attend Kalani High School if her parents wished. The Department also informed Rachel's father that, should he enroll her in private school, such enrollment would be considered a unilateral placement at parents expense."

"The Department never proposed a new IEP meeting in light of the family's move. Nor did it ever identify a school in Kailua that could meet Rachel's special education needs. It did, however, repeatedly ask for the family's new address. Rachel's father ignored these requests until January 2013, when, in addition to giving the Department the family's new address, he filed a due process hearing request on behalf of Rachel, arguing that the Department had denied Rachel a FAPE by not identifying the anticipated school where Rachel's IEP would be implemented. He did not raise any substantive challenge to Rachel's IEP. In response, the Department argued it had complied with the IDEA's requirements and that Rachel's IEP could be implemented on a public school campus."

The Hearing Officer agreed. The parents appealed to the U.S. District Court which held that "an IEP need not necessarily identify a specific school where it would be implemented to comply with the IDEA. Rachel timely appealed."

The Ninth Circuit explained that "This appeal concerns the meaning of 'location' in §1414(d)(1)(A)(i)(VII). If, as Rachel's father argues, 'location' means the specific school where an IEP will be implemented, then at the beginning of the 2012-13 school year the Department failed to have in place an IEP that identified an anticipated school in Kailua, Rachel's new home town, where special education services would be delivered. If, on the other hand, location does not mean the specific school, then the district court correctly affirmed dismissal of Rachel's claims. We hold location does not necessarily include the specific school where special education services will be implemented. We therefore affirm."

(Parent's Attorney – Jay S. Handlin // School's Attorney – Kaliko'onalani D. Fernandes)

Outcome: Hawaii DOE prevailed.

R.E.B. v. Hawaii DOE
9th Cir.
870 F.3d 1025
9/13/2017 – Hawaii

This is a private school tuition reimbursement case with legal issues related to mootness, transition, IEP specificity, LRE, and ABA "methodology."

The parent lost before the HO and district court.

The Ninth Circuit opened with this:

"Before and during this lawsuit, J.B. attended the Pacific Autism Center ('PAC'), a small private school for students with autism and other special needs. During that time, Hawaii Department of Education ('DOE') personnel convened to develop an Individualized Education Plan ('IEP') for J.B.'s transition from PAC into public kindergarten. J.B. raised various objections to aspects of the proposed IEP, but the presiding administrative hearings officer found that the IEP was adequate. J.B.

appeals from the district court's affirmation of that determination."

The Ninth Circuit noted that: "DOE claims this case is now moot because J.B. received relief beyond that originally requested. J.B. initially sought reimbursement of PAC tuition for the 2012-13 school year, and DOE funded J.B.'s tuition at PAC from 2012 until 2015. [Presumably pursuant to "Stay Put."] But a case is moot only when it is impossible for a court to grant any effectual relief whatever to the prevailing party.
[Citation omitted.] J.B.'s due process complaint sought reimbursement for transportation and compensatory education, in addition to reimbursement for tuition at PAC. Because we can still grant effectual relief, this case is not moot."

The father asserted that the Hearing Officer and the U.S. District Court used a narrow definition of transition services and that it should also include transition from "PAC to a public school." The Ninth Circuit agreed, explaining that opinions in the past "have read the IDEA too narrowly and are to that extent overruled."

"Where transition services become necessary for disabled children to 'be educated and participate' in new academic environments, transition services must be included in IEPs in order to satisfy the IDEA's supplementary aids and services requirement."

The IEP failed to specify "the Least Restrictive Environment (LRE) during the regular and extended school year." In its criticism of the IEP, the Court noted that "the language was also too vague to enable J.B. to use the IEP as a blueprint for enforcement."

"Moreover, the IEP didn't detail the anticipated frequency, location, and duration of the proposed specialized instruction in J.B.'s Science and Social Studies activities, as required by 34 C.F.R. § 300.320(a)(7). This fails to meet the legally required threshold of specificity."

"DOE's cursory treatment of the *Rachel H.* factors was demonstrated by J.B.'s being mainstreamed into Mandarin — a class obviously inappropriate for him — but not into Science or Social Studies. This seriously infringed J.B.'s father's opportunity to participate in the IEP process and was therefore a denial of a FAPE."

(**Wrightslaw Note:** *Rachel H.* is a landmark 1994 Ninth Circuit case which describes the elements of LRE.)

"Finally, J.B. argues that DOE violated the IDEA by failing to specify Applied Behavioral Analysis (ABA) as a methodology in the IEP."

"The IEP team discussed ABA at length and recognized that it was integral to J.B.'s education. And ABA is widely recognized as a superior method for teaching children with autism. [Citations omitted.] When a particular methodology plays a critical role in the student's educational plan, it must be specified in the IEP rather than left up to individual teachers' discretion."

"[S]pecifying ABA in writing would not have precluded the use of other methodologies. It simply would have ensured that ABA would be consistently used in J.B.'s educational program, since even the school district acknowledged that ABA should be part of J.B.'s education. The IEP's failure to specify ABA was thus a denial of a FAPE."

There was a strong dissent from Circuit Judge Bea to the Per Curiam decision. The other two panelists were Circuit Judges Kozinski and Hawkins.

The Court reversed the U.S. District Court and remanded back "to the district court for determination of the appropriate remedy."

(Parent's Attorney - Keith H.S. Peck // School's Attorney – Gary S. Suganuma)

Initial Outcome: The parent prevailed, however Hawaii filed a Petition for a Panel Rehearing. On

April 3, 2018, the "Opinion and dissent filed on September 13, 2017, are withdrawn, and this case is resubmitted pending further order of this court." **There is no final outcome at this point**. The case is still pending awaiting further briefs and possible Oral Argument.

J.S. v. Houston County Bd. Ed.
11th Cir.
10/2/2017 – Alabama

This is a **Wrightslaw Case of the Year.** We encourage lay advocates and special education attorneys to read it.

This case against the school board claims that, by acting unlawfully or by failing to act, "the HCBOE deprived J.S., III of the required supervision and services required by law, excluded him from and denied him the benefits of public, federally supported programs and facilities operated by HCBOE, and, ultimately, led to and caused his discrimination and harassment."

It includes issues such as a *Fry* allegation of failure to exhaust, physical abuse of a child, and violations of Section 504 and the Americans with Disabilities Act.

In *J.S. v. Houston*, the Alabama parents filed Section 504 and ADA claims against various school teachers, coaches, and the school board pursuant to alleged abuse of their child who has "severe physical disabilities and cognitive impairments."

The U.S. District Court dismissed the case. The parents appealed.

The Eleventh Circuit noted that "When J.S. was in the third grade (2010 to 2011) and fourth grade (2011 to 2012), he received individual education plans (IEPs), under which he was assigned to regular and special education classrooms. The IEPs noted that J.S. had poor balance, used a walker and a wheelchair at school, needed help with using the

restroom, and received physical and occupational services while at school."

"The IEPs specified that J.S. was to spend 80 percent of his time in the regular classroom and 20 percent of his time in the special education classroom. Alicia Brown was J.S.' special education teacher during his third-grade year and part of his fourth-grade year and Angie Boatright was his regular classroom teacher during his fourth-grade year. Drew Faircloth was assigned to work with J.S. as a teacher's aide/special education paraprofessional starting J.S.' third-grade year. Mr. Faircloth helped J.S. with going to the restroom, getting around the school campus, going to lunch and recess, participating in physical education, and completing class work."

"In late 2011 and early 2012, Mr. Faircloth began taking J.S. out of his regular classroom and bringing him to the school's weight room, purportedly because J.S. was disruptive in the classroom and because they could do physical therapy and use the private restroom there. Ms. Boatright testified that she never instructed Mr. Faircloth to take J.S. out of the classroom for being a distraction to others or being distracted himself."

"Principal Smith testified that she spoke with Mr. Faircloth and asked him to stop taking J.S. to the weight room. Mr. Faircloth continued to remove J.S. from the classroom."

"In March of 2012, a fellow student, R.T., witnessed Mr. Faircloth kick J.S.' wheelchair, while telling him to be quiet, refusing to pick up his pencil for him, and otherwise berating him. R.T. told her parents, who then informed J.S.' parents about what R.T. had witnessed. In response, J.S.' parents placed an audio recorder underneath J.S.' wheelchair for several days. According to J.S.' parents, the device captured verbal abuse by Mr. Faircloth and Ms. Brown, and possible physical abuse by Mr. Faircloth."

"J.S.' parents contacted the school district's special education coordinator, Denise Whitfield, to report what they had heard on the recordings. Mr. Faircloth and Ms. Brown were placed on administrative leave and received written reprimands from Principal Smith. Mr. Faircloth ultimately resigned from his position and the School Board decided not to renew Ms. Brown's contract."

"J.S., through his parents, originally filed an action in 2012 against the School Board, Mr. Faircloth, Ms. Brown, and others. He settled his claims against Mr. Faircloth and Ms. Brown. The district court granted summary judgment to the School Board because J.S. had failed to exhaust his administrative remedies but dismissed the suit without prejudice. J.S. subsequently filed an administrative due process complaint with the Alabama Department of Education pursuant to the Individuals with Disabilities Education Act, 20 U.S.C. § 1400 *et seq.*, and J.S. and the School Board resolved that dispute. J.S. then filed this action against the School Board, alleging Title II and § 504 violations relating to his removal from the classroom and the verbal and physical abuse."

"The district court granted summary judgment in favor of the School Board, concluding that (1) regarding his removal from the classroom, J.S. had not shown more than a failure to provide a free appropriate public education (FAPE) under the IDEA; and (2) J.S. had not provided any evidence that the School Board had notice of future verbal and physical abuse. This appeal followed."

"J.S. argues that the district court erred by mischaracterizing his Title II and § 504 claim regarding his removal from his regular classroom as merely a claim that he was denied a FAPE, a right guaranteed under the IDEA."

"J.S. has alleged—and has provided evidence tending to show—that he was, with some frequency, excluded and isolated from his classroom and peers on the basis of his disability. Although the circumstances alleged here do involve a violation of J.S.' IEP, they also implicate those

further, intangible consequences of discrimination contemplated in *Olmstead* that could result from isolation, such as stigmatization and deprivation of opportunities for enriching interaction with fellow students. These injuries reach beyond a misdiagnosis or failure to provide appropriate remedial coursework."

"[T]he district court erred in analyzing this claim as merely a FAPE violation under the IDEA."

The Court of Appeals concluded that "J.S. has stated a claim of intentional discrimination" and then proceeded to analyze who might be the potential defendants. The Court concluded that "a jury could find that Principal Smith was deliberately indifferent" as well as teachers Boatwright and Brown. It appears that the special education coordinator, Whitfield, escaped liability because she was not deliberately indifferent and took action.

The Court of Appeals affirmed the dismissal of the case against the two coaches and reversed the dismissal against the other defendants and remanded the case back to the U.S. District Court for further proceedings. Unless settled, this will probably lead to a jury trial similar to *Ebonie S.* discussed below.

Pursuant to a March, 2018 review of the U.S. District Court's Docket Sheet, this case is being prepared for a jury trial.)

(**Wrightslaw Note:** The Complaint filed in the U.S. District Court on December 3, 2014 is located on our website at:

http://www.wrightslaw.com/law/pleadings/AL.houston.complaint.jury.pdf

(**Wrightslaw Note:** Issues in this case are similar to the *Ebonie S. v. Pueblo Sch. Dist.* case in Colorado that was featured in our 2015 Year in Review book and is our website. Ebonie was restrained in a desk chair structure, similar to a Rifton Chair. A jury found that such restraints were not used with children who did not have disabilities and, as a result, for this Section 504 violation, awarded two million, two hundred thousand dollars, ($2,200,000.00) to the parents, which was upheld on appeal. Click here for *Ebonie S.* Jury Instructions and Jury Verdict located on our Wrightslaw.com website.)

(Parent's Attorney – William T. "Bo" Johnson // School's Attorney – James Kevin Walding)

Outcome: Parents prevailed.

N.B. v. NYC DOE
2ⁿᵈ Cir.
10/10/2017 – New York

This is a tuition reimbursement case for a child with autism. It includes issues of methodology, deference, and student teacher ratio. The parents rejected the school district's proposed "P369K" placement and sought tuition reimbursement for a private school which provided "DIR/Floortime" as the "means of achieving progress."

In an unusual decision, "the IHO found that any procedural defects in developing the IEP were *de minimis,* but that H.B. was denied a FAPE because the Department had failed to offer the IEP into evidence at the hearing. The IHO nonetheless found that the Parents lacked standing to seek tuition reimbursement because their contract with the private school was illusory."

"Both the Department and the Parents appealed the IHO's ruling to a State Review Officer (SRO). On February 26, 2015, the SRO reversed the IHO, finding that the IEP was properly in evidence and the Parents had standing to seek tuition reimbursement. As to the merits of the dispute, the SRO determined that the IEP was sufficient and offered H.B. a FAPE."

The Parents appealed to the U.S. District Court. "The parties filed motions for summary judgment ...

[and] the district court granted summary judgment in favor of the Department."

On appeal before the Second Circuit "the Parents raise no procedural objections and instead challenge the SRO's substantive conclusion that H.B. was offered a FAPE. The Parents principally argue the SRO's decision was insufficiently reasoned or supported for the following reasons: (1) the IEP was inappropriate because it did not expressly prescribe the method of instruction or goals established at H.B.'s private school ('DIR/Floortime') and (2) the student to teacher classroom ratio recommended in the IEP and school facility designated by the Department were not equipped to implement DIR/Floortime such that H.B. could make progress toward those goals. The Parents further argue the overall environment at ... P369K ... was inappropriate for H.B. and inconsistent with the IEP because it would subject her to an environment that would have been intolerable due to her severe autism and the school's inability to provide for her dietary needs."

"We are not persuaded. To the extent the Parents' challenges concern the substantive merits of the IEP's recommendations and P369K's ability to implement those recommendations, we must defer to the SRO's expertise and decision. As to the Parents' first argument, we agree with the Parents and the district court that the IEP implicitly recommended the DIR/Floortime method by adopting the language and overall goals set by H.B.'s private school. We agree, however, that the SRO reasonably concluded that the IEP goals did not specifically mandate DIR/Floortime to achieve such goals, and instead reflected commonly used tenets of special education instruction, regardless of methodology employed. The SRO reasonably rejected the assertion that DIR/Floortime is the only means of achieving progress such that the IEP's failure to mandate DIR/Floortime amounts to a denial of a FAPE."

"We also defer to the SRO's conclusion that the student to teacher ratio adopted by the IEP was sufficient to meet H.B.'s needs."

"Therefore, we affirm the SRO's — and the district court's — decision that the Parents are not entitled to reimbursement of H.B.'s private school tuition."

(Parent's Attorney – Steven Goldstein // School's Attorney – Daniel Matza-Brown)

Outcome: School prevailed.

H.E. v. Walter Palmer Charter Sch. + PA DOE
3rd Cir.
873 F.3d 406
Circuit Judge Krause
10/11/2017 - Pennsylvania

This convoluted attorney's fee case that has some legal similarities to the Third Circuit's decision in *M.R. v. Ridley*, authored by the same Circuit Judge and issued on August 22, 2017. However, the facts are quite different.

The parents' three children were initially enrolled in a Charter School, which failed to provide the children with FAPE. "In 2014, after negotiations with Plaintiffs and their attorneys, the Charter School entered with Plaintiffs into settlement agreements that fully resolved Plaintiffs' IDEA claims. Under these agreements, the Charter School was to fund a number of hours of compensatory education for each child and to contribute towards Plaintiffs' attorneys' fees."

"But the Charter School permanently closed in December 2014 and never delivered on its obligations under the settlement agreements. In response, Plaintiffs filed administrative due process complaints with the Pennsylvania Department of Education, naming both the Charter School and the Department of Education as defendants."

"[T]he administrative hearing officer promptly dismissed the complaints, opining that, rather than

seek compensatory education from the Department as an entity ultimately responsible for their children's education, *id.*, Plaintiffs were required to enforce their settlement agreements with the Charter School through the Charter School's settlement-of-claims process."

"Plaintiffs then filed suit against the Charter School and the Department in federal court, seeking reversal of the administrative decisions dismissing their claims under the IDEA, remand to the administrative hearing officer, and an award of attorneys' fees and costs. Ultimately, aside from the requested award of attorneys' fees and costs, Plaintiffs obtained all of the relief they had sought. The District Court vacated the hearing officer's decisions and remanded Plaintiffs' compensatory education claims to the hearing officer for a due process hearing, explaining that the hearing officer had erred as a matter of law."

"On remand, Plaintiffs and the Department agreed on the number of hours of compensatory education owed to Plaintiffs' children, but, because they disagreed about the hourly rate applicable to the Department's compensatory education payments, the hearing officer issued a decision setting the applicable rate."

"Plaintiffs filed a motion for attorneys' fees in this case, citing their successful bids for reversal and remand with respect to the hearing officer's initial decision dismissing their administrative complaints. The District Court denied the motion, explaining that its grant of summary judgment did not address whether Plaintiffs ultimately would succeed on their substantive claims against the Department, but instead was confined to purely procedural matters. The District Court reasoned that Plaintiffs therefore were not prevailing parties, and, as a result, it lacked discretion to award Plaintiffs any fee award."

"Plaintiffs contend that they in fact were prevailing parties for purposes of the IDEA's attorneys' fees provision and that they therefore were eligible for a fee award. Our precedent compels us to agree ... if a parent vindicates a procedural right guaranteed by the IDEA, and if the relief she obtains is not temporary forward-looking injunctive relief, then she is a prevailing party under the IDEA attorneys' fee provision and is eligible for an award of attorneys' fees, 20 U.S.C. § 1415(i)(3)(B)(i). Particularly given the importance Congress attached to the IDEA's procedural safeguards, *Rowley*, 458 U.S. at 205, 102 S.Ct. 3034, we readily conclude that even a purely procedural victory under the IDEA can confer prevailing party status."

The Court of Appeals reversed and remanded for a determination and calculation of fees to be awarded to the parents.

(Parent's Attorney – David J. Berney // School's Attorney – John G. Knorr, III)

Outcome: Parents prevailed.

R.C. v. Wappingers Bd. Ed. Cent. Sch. Dist.
2nd Cir.

12/1/2017 – New York

In this tuition reimbursement case, the IHO ruled in favor of the parents. The school district appealed. The SRO ruled in favor of the school district. The parents appealed to the U.S. District Court, which also ruled in favor of the school district. The parents appealed to the Second Circuit.

The Second Circuit discussed the *Burlington/Carter* test to determine if the private placement justifies reimbursement to the parents.

"Though this Court typically engages in a de novo review of decisions regarding summary judgment, the standard of review is modified in the context of administrative agency decisions under IDEA. Instead, the reviewing court is tasked with an analysis that this Court has termed a circumscribed de novo review ... because the responsibility for determining whether a challenged IEP will provide a child with a FAPE rests in the first instance with administrative hearing and review officers. [Citation omitted.] When the IHO and SRO disagree, a reviewing court generally should defer to the final decision of the state authorities, that is, the SRO's decision. In the ordinary case, it is not for the federal court to choose between the views of conflicting experts on such questions. [Citation omitted.] We turn to the IHO decision only if the SRO decision is unpersuasive even after appropriate deference is paid." [Citation omitted.]

"In the case of a unilateral parental placement in a private school, the parents' entitlement to reimbursement is assessed under the three-step *Burlington/Carter* test: (1) the DOE must establish that the student's IEP actually provided a FAPE; should the DOE fail to meet that burden, the parents are entitled to reimbursement if (2) they establish that their unilateral placement was appropriate and (3) the equities favor them. [Citation omitted.] Under the circumscribed *de novo* review of IDEA claims, *id.*, this Court is thus tasked with independently verifying the determination of the SRO regarding the sufficiency of the proposed IEP and the unilateral placement. *Id.*"

"The IHO and SRO disagreed on each of the first two prongs of the *Burlington/Carter* three-step analysis. ... Accordingly, we must assess whether the SRO decision was sufficiently reasoned and supported by the record to merit deference." [Citation omitted.]

"We agree with the district court that the SRO's decision is supported by a preponderance of the evidence and deserves deference. [Citation omitted.] ... The SRO also addressed the fact that the school district's recommended placement was a day program, while the parents' unilateral placement was a residential program. The SRO found that the recommended placement struck an appropriate balance between N.C.'s therapeutic needs and the statutory directive requiring CSE's to offer a placement in the least restrictive environment."

"We find the SRO's decision to be thorough and well-reasoned ... the IHO's analysis was markedly less persuasive than that of the SRO, insofar as it relied on fewer sources of evidence and did not engage in a holistic assessment of the entire record, as opposed to relying heavily on the testimony and impressions of N.C.'s parents. Most significantly, the IHO did not thoroughly address the attributes of the private placement, apart from his discussion regarding aesthetic concerns. ... Accordingly, this Court will defer to the well-reasoned opinion of the SRO that is supported by a preponderance of the evidence."

(Parent's Attorney – Benjamin J. Hinerfeld // School's Attorney – Neelanjan Choudhury)

Outcome: Second Circuit upheld the U.S. District Court, tuition reimbursement denied, school prevailed.

N.P. v. Prince George's County Bd. Ed. + Maxwell
4th Cir.
Circuit Judge Wynn
12/8/2017 - Maryland

This tuition reimbursement case was affected, in mid-stream, by the SCOTUS ruling in *Endrew F.* issued on March 22, 2017.

The relevant background is that "The ALJ found in favor of the school system, and N.P.'s parents subsequently appealed to the district court. The district court did not conduct any further evidentiary hearings but instead reversed the ALJ based on the record from the administrative proceedings. The school system timely appealed to this Court."

The Fourth Circuit was quite critical of district court's decision and explained that:

"After N.P.'s parents appealed to the district court, the district court provided a slightly more than three-page opinion setting forth six reasons why it disagreed with the ALJ. Those six reasons provide scant detail and insight into the district court's thought process and are not supported by a single case citation. Most importantly, the district court did not explain its complete deviation from the ALJ's factual findings."

"As the opinion stands, the district court provided no substantive reasons why it discounted the ALJ's findings regarding the standardized test results, especially given that the ALJ's conclusions were based on the opinions of professional educators. This same error—reversing the ALJ's factual findings without giving adequate explanations as to why—occurs throughout the district court's opinion."

"The other major shortcoming of the district court's opinion is related: the district court consistently rejected the ALJ's credibility determinations without describing what led it to do so."

"None of the above should call into question the authority of a district court to disagree with an ALJ's findings. Congress included judicial review in the statute for a purpose. Yet if a district court is going to disagree with regularly made factual findings, then it must 'explain how it, despite the fact that it was reviewing a cold record, reached a conclusion completely contrary to that of the ALJ, who conducted the proceedings.' In so doing, the district court 'should address each such relevant factual finding made by the hearing officer and explain why, under the due weight standard, it has chosen to accept or not accept that finding.' [Citation omitted.] The district court in this case did not meet that standard."

"Having determined the district court's opinion did not give due weight to the administrative findings, we next must decide the appropriate remedy. When reversing a district court in similar cases, we have sometimes remanded for further proceedings and other times decided the case ourselves based upon the record. [Citation omitted.] In this case, remand is prudent because, during the pendency of this appeal, the Supreme Court clarified the standard for assessing whether a disabled pupil received a free appropriate public education."

"[T]his case was originally placed in abeyance until the Supreme Court released its opinion in *Endrew F.* Prior to *Endrew*, the seminal case regarding a free appropriate public education was *Board of Education v. Rowley*, 458 U.S. 176 (1982). In that case, the Court said a free appropriate public education must be sufficient to confer some educational benefit. *Id.* at 200. Some courts of appeal had subsequently interpreted that standard to mean the educational benefit mandated by [the] IDEA must merely be more than de minimis. *Endrew F. ex rel. Joseph F. v. Douglas Cty. Sch. Dist. RE-1*, 798 F.3d 1329, 1338 (10th Cir. 2015) (internal quotation marks omitted), rev'd, *Endrew*, 137 S. Ct. 988. In *Endrew F.*, the Supreme Court invalidated that interpretation. Rather, the Court articulated a new standard: 'To meet its substantive obligation under the IDEA, a school must offer an IEP reasonably calculated to enable a child to make progress appropriate in light of the child's circumstances.'"
Endrew, 137 S. Ct. at 999.

"We need not fully explore the impact of *Endrew* in this case, however. Both the ALJ and the district court wrote their opinions prior to *Endrew*. In fact, the ALJ quotes the more than de minimis standard in her opinion. The ALJ—the only person to see the witnesses testify in person—should have the opportunity to decide in the first instance whether the outcome of the case is different under the standard articulated by the Supreme Court in *Endrew*. We therefore remand to the district court so it can order further proceedings consistent with this opinion."

(**Wrightslaw Note**: Update as of March 2018 - this case is now before the ALJ with briefing and oral argument pending.)

(Parent's Attorney - Michael Eig // School's Attorney - Andrew Wayne Nussbaum // COPAA Amicus Attorney - Selene Almazan-Altobelli))

Outcome: A draw. Remanded back for reconsideration in light of the decision in *Endrew F.*

Wellman v. Butler Area Sch. Dist.
3rd Cir.
Circuit Judge Shwartz
12/12/2017 – Pennsylvania

On February 22, 2017, the U.S. Supreme Court issued *Fry,* a decision about when a case must be "exhausted" prior to filing suit in the U.S. District Court. If there is a special education dispute and "a plaintiff seeks relief for 'denial of the IDEA's core guarantee [of] ... a free and appropriate education [FAPE,]' [Citation omitted] ... then the plaintiff must exhaust his administrative remedies under the IDEA."

Fry is central to this case.

Wellman "suffered a head injury while playing flag football in his freshman physical education class. After school that day, Wellman attended football practice, where he suffered additional head injuries. The following day, Wellman saw his doctor and later underwent a CT scan, which revealed that he had sustained a concussion. Wellman suffered 'pain' and experienced 'staring spells, trouble sleeping, and difficulty concentrating.'" At that time, Wellman was not a child with a disability and did not have either an IEP or Section 504 Plan.

"After performing an EEG test, Wellman's doctor wrote a letter asking the school to provide Wellman with academic accommodations, specifically tutors and more time to complete his assignments. The school ignored these requests."

Thereafter Wellman suffered another concussion while holding sideline markers during a football game and his "symptoms worsened, and he experienced severe headaches, problems focusing, and exhaustion. A CT scan revealed that he had post-concussive syndrome. Wellman began to miss school because of his symptoms and medical appointments, and when he was able to attend school, his teachers refused to provide accommodations for him. As a result, Wellman suffered significant stress, embarrassment, and anxiety."

Wellman's mother "requested that he be evaluated for an Individualized Education Plan ('IEP'). The school determined that Wellman was not eligible for an IEP. ... The school proposed a 'Chapter 15/504 plan' to help Wellman return to school, but the parties could not reach an agreement on its implementation. Four months later, they met again to discuss a Chapter 15/504 plan, but school officials appeared uninterested in giving Wellman 'any sort of accommodations.' Wellman finished his sophomore year in cyber school. The following year, he enrolled in private school, from which he eventually graduated."

"Wellman and his parents filed a due process complaint with the Pennsylvania Department of Education against the School District, requesting a hearing, an IEP, compensatory education for two years, and payment of Wellman's private school tuition. Wellman and the School District eventually entered into a Settlement and Release Agreement [which] ... released the School District and its employees 'from all rights, claims, causes of action, and damages of any nature including, but not limited to, any claim for legal fees and/or costs, which were pursued in the above-referenced case or which could have been pursued in the above-referenced case, pursuant to the IDEA, as amended; the Americans with Disabilities Act (ADA); or any

other Federal or State statute, including the regulations promulgated thereunder.'"

Then the parents sued the "School District and the high school's principal," alleging violations of Section 504 and the ADA.

The U.S. District Court "dismissed the Complaint without prejudice, because (1) each of Wellman's claims were related to the provision of a FAPE, and he failed to exhaust his claims before a special education hearing officer ... (3) no exception to exhaustion was applicable to the case . . ."

(**Wrightslaw Note:** Without prejudice permits a refiling of the case, subject to revisions to the Complaint. Query – Unaddressed in the Opinion is the impact of the prior settlement agreement – could this have been a factor leading to dismissal?)

On appeal, the Third Circuit, pursuant to *Fry*, said "What matters is the crux— or, in legal speak, the gravamen—of the plaintiff's complaint."

"Application of the *Fry* framework to Wellman's entire complaint and each of his claims shows that his grievances all stem from the alleged failure to accommodate his condition and fulfill his educational needs." In this instance "he cannot cure the defect in his complaint."

"As a result, we will vacate the District Court's order dismissing the complaint without prejudice and remand with instructions to dismiss the complaint with prejudice."

(**Wrightslaw Note:** In 1995, the Third Circuit issued a dollar damage case that shook the special education legal community. In *WB v. Matula*, 67 F.3d. 484, 494 (3d Cir.1995) the Court held that "money damages were available in a §1983 action based on an IDEA violation." Later, in *A.W. v. Jersey City Public Schools*, 486 F.3d 791 (3d Cir.2007) the Court diluted Matula and held that because "IDEA provides a comprehensive remedial scheme, Congress did not intend § 1983 to be available to remedy violations of the IDEA." Since then, the pendulum in the Third Circuit has continued to swing in the direction of eliminating potential dollar damage, jury trials in any school case that could have disability overtones.

Compare this case to the October 2, 2017 *J.S. v. Houston County Bd. Ed.* case of the year which had a similar legal process, but opposite outcome.)

(Parent's Attorney – Edward A. Olds // School's Attorney – Thomas E. Breth)

Outcome: School district prevailed, case dismissed with prejudice.

J.P. v. NYC DOE

2nd Cir.

12/19/2017 – New York

This is a tuition reimbursement case about deference owed to the earlier decisions and the school district's failure to conduct a Functional Behavior Assessment (FBA) and provide a Behavior Intervention Plan (BIP).

The parents argued that the "DOE failed to conduct an adequate functional behavioral assessment (FBA) or develop an adequate behavioral intervention plan (BIP)" and that the "public school placement under the IEP was predetermined, impeding their opportunity to meaningfully participate in the decision-making process."

The parents lost at the due process hearing and at review. Their U.S. District Court appeal was also unsuccessful. They appealed to the Second Circuit.

The Second Circuit explained that "the question is whether the IEP is reasonable, not whether the court regards it as ideal. [Citation omitted.] On this question, substantial deference is owed to the judgments of state administrators. [Citation omitted.] ... Like the District Court, we conclude that the IHO's and SRO's decisions merit deference because they are well reasoned and supported by the record."

The Court explained that "Although the failure to conduct an FBA or BIP in conformity with New York State regulations is a serious procedural violation, it does not rise to the level of a denial of a FAPE if the IEP adequately identifies the problem behavior and prescribes ways to manage it. [Citation omitted.] We agree with the IHO and SRO that the 2013-2014 IEP adequately identified J.P.'s problem behaviors, including his inattention and impulsivity, and addressed those behaviors with the provision of a 1:1 paraprofessional and related services. Therefore, even assuming that the DOE failed to fully comply with State regulations, that failure would not automatically deny J.P. a FAPE."

The parents argued that "J.P.'s public school placement under the IEP was predetermined, impeding their opportunity to meaningfully participate in the decisionmaking process. Although parents are denied meaningful participation when the school district lacks an open mind as to the contents of a child's IEP, [citation omitted] J.P.'s parents have failed to make this showing. The record demonstrates that the CSE heard their objections, considered materials they submitted, and convened a second meeting to address their objections and explain its reasoning, and that J.P.'s parents fully participated in both CSE meetings."

"Because J.P.'s IEP was substantively and procedurally adequate, we need not address whether his private placement was appropriate or whether the equitable factors favor reimbursement."

"We have considered the parents' remaining arguments and conclude that they are without merit. For the foregoing reasons, the judgment of the District Court is affirmed."

(Parent's Attorney – Theresa Scotto-Lavino // School's Attorney – Devin Slack)

Outcome: Tuition reimbursement denied, school prevailed.

END of Case Summaries

Below are hyperlinks to the prior chapter.
[e-book PDF download version only]

Chapter 6. Supreme Court Decisions: *Fry v. Napoleon & Endrew F. v. Douglas Co.*

Stacy Fry et vir, as next friends of minor E. F.

v.

Napoleon Community Schools, et al.

OPINION OF THE COURT

No. 15–497

Argued October 31, 2016 - Decided February 22, 2017

JUSTICE KAGAN delivered the opinion of the Court.

The Individuals with Disabilities Education Act (IDEA or Act), 84 Stat. 175, as amended, 20 U.S.C. §1400 *et seq*., ensures that children with disabilities receive needed special education services. One of its provisions, §1415(l), addresses the Act's relationship with other laws protecting those children. Section 1415(l) makes clear that nothing in the IDEA "restrict[s] or limit[s] the rights [or] remedies" that other federal laws, including antidiscrimination statutes, confer on children with disabilities. At the same time, the section states that if a suit brought under such a law "seek[s] relief that is also available under" the IDEA, the plaintiff must first exhaust the IDEA's administrative procedures. In this case, we consider the scope of

that exhaustion requirement. We hold that exhaustion is not necessary when the gravamen of the plaintiff's suit is something other than the denial of the IDEA's core guarantee—what the Act calls a "free appropriate public education." §1412(a)(1)(A).

I

A

The IDEA offers federal funds to States in exchange for a commitment: to furnish a "free appropriate public education"—more concisely known as a FAPE—to all children with certain physical or intellectual disabilities. *Ibid.*; see §1401(3)(A)(i) (listing covered disabilities). As defined in the Act, a FAPE comprises "special education and related services"—both "instruction" tailored to meet a child's "unique needs" and sufficient "supportive services" to permit the child to benefit from that instruction. §§1401(9), (26), (29); see *Board of Ed. of Hendrick Hudson Central School Dist., Westchester Cty. v. Rowley*, 458 U.S.176, 203 (1982). An eligible child, as this Court has explained, acquires a "substantive right" to such an education once a State accepts the IDEA's financial assistance. *Smith v. Robinson*, 468 U.S.992, 1010 (1984).

Under the IDEA, an "individualized education pro-gram," called an IEP for short, serves as the "primary vehicle" for providing each child with the promised FAPE. *Honig v. Doe*, 484 U.S.305, 311 (1988); see §1414(d). (Welcome to—and apologies for—the acronymic world of federal legislation.) Crafted by a child's "IEP Team"—a group of school officials, teachers, and parents—the IEP spells out a personalized plan to meet all of the child's "educational needs." §§1414(d)(1)(A)(i)(II)(bb), (d)(1)(B). Most notably, the IEP documents the child's current "levels of academic achievement," specifies "measurable annual goals" for how she can "make progress in the general education curriculum," and lists the "special education and related services" to be provided so that she can "advance appropriately toward [those] goals." §§1414(d)(1)(A)(i)(I), (II), (IV)(aa).

Because parents and school representatives sometimes cannot agree on such issues, the IDEA establishes formal procedures for resolving disputes. To begin, a dissatisfied parent may file a complaint as to any matter concerning the provision of a FAPE with the local or state educational agency (as state law provides). See §1415(b)(6). That pleading generally triggers a "[p]reliminary meeting" involving the contending parties, §1415(f)(1)(B)(i); at their option, the parties may instead (or also) pursue a full-fledged mediation process, see §1415(e). Assuming their impasse continues, the matter proceeds to a "due process hearing" before an impartial hearing officer. §1415(f)(1)(A); see §1415(f)(3)(A)(i). Any decision of the officer granting substantive relief must be "based on a determination of whether the child received a [FAPE]." §1415(f)(3)(E)(i). If the hearing is initially conducted at the local level, the ruling is appealable to the state agency. See §1415(g). Finally, a parent unhappy with the outcome of the administrative process may seek judicial review by filing a civil action in state or federal court. See §1415(i)(2)(A).

Important as the IDEA is for children with disabilities, it is not the only federal statute protecting their interests. Of particular relevance to this case are two antidiscrimination laws—Title II of the Americans with Disabilities Act (ADA), 42 U.S.C. §12131 *et seq.*, and §504 of the Rehabilitation Act, 29 U. S. C. §794—which cover both adults and children with disabilities, in both public schools and other settings. Title II forbids any "public entity" from discriminating based on disability; Section 504 applies the same prohibition to any federally funded "pro- gram or activity." 42 U. S. C. §§12131–12132; 29 U. S. C. §794(a). A regulation implementing Title II requires a public entity to make "reasonable modifications" to its "policies, practices, or procedures" when necessary to avoid such discrimination. 28 CFR §35.130(b)(7) (2016); see, e.g., *Alboniga v. School Bd. of Broward Cty.*, 87 F. Supp. 3d 1319, 1345 (SD Fla. 2015) (requiring an accommodation to permit use of a service animal under Title II). In similar vein, courts have interpreted §504 as demanding certain "reasonable" modifications to existing practices in order to "accommodate" persons with disabilities. *Alexander v. Choate*, 469 U. S. 287, 299–300 (1985); see, e.g., *Sullivan v. Vallejo City Unified School Dist.*, 731 F. Supp. 947, 961–962 (ED Cal. 1990) (requiring an accommodation to permit use of a service animal under §504). And both statutes authorize individuals to seek redress for violations of their substantive guarantees by bringing suits for injunctive relief or money damages. See 29 U. S. C. §794a(a)(2); 42 U. S. C. §12133.

This Court first considered the interaction between such laws and the IDEA in Smith v. Robinson, 468 U. S. 992. (Footnote 1) The plaintiffs there sought "to secure a 'free appropriate public education' for [their] handicapped child." Id., at 994. But instead of bringing suit under the IDEA alone, they appended "virtually identical" claims (again alleging the denial of a "free appropriate public education") under §504 of the Rehabilitation Act and the Fourteenth Amendment's Equal Protection Clause. Id., at 1009; see Id., at 1016. The Court held that the IDEA altogether foreclosed those additional claims: With its "comprehensive" and "carefully tailored" provisions, the Act was "the exclusive avenue" through which a child with a disability (or his parents) could challenge the adequacy of his education. Id., at 1009; see Id., at 1013, 1016, 1021.

Congress was quick to respond. In the Handicapped Children's Protection Act of 1986, 100 Stat. 796, it over- turned *Smith's* preclusion of non-IDEA claims while also adding a carefully defined exhaustion requirement. Now codified at 20 U. S. C. §1415(l), the relevant provision of that statute reads:

"Nothing in [the IDEA] shall be construed to restrict or limit the rights, procedures, and remedies available under the Constitution, the [ADA], title V of the Re- habilitation Act [including §504], or other Federal laws protecting the rights of children with disabilities, except that before the filing of a civil action under such laws seeking relief that is also available under [the IDEA], the [IDEA's administrative procedures] shall be exhausted to the same extent as would be required had the action been brought under [the IDEA]."

The first half of §1415(l) (up until "except that") "reaffirm[s] the viability" of federal statutes like the ADA or Rehabilitation Act "as separate vehicles,"

no less integral than the IDEA, "for ensuring the rights of handicapped children." H. R. Rep. No. 99– 296, p. 4 (1985); see *Id.,* at 6. According to that opening phrase, the IDEA does not prevent a plaintiff from asserting claims under such laws even if, as in Smith itself, those claims allege the denial of an appropriate public education (much as an IDEA claim would). But the second half of §1415(l) (from "except that" onward) imposes a limit on that "anything goes" regime, in the form of an exhaustion provision. According to that closing phrase, a plaintiff bringing suit under the ADA, the Rehabilitation Act, or similar laws must in certain circumstances—that is, when "seeking relief that is also available under" the IDEA—first exhaust the IDEA's administrative procedures. The reach of that requirement is the issue in this case.

B

Petitioner E. F. is a child with a severe form of cerebral palsy, which "significantly limits her motor skills and mobility." App. to Brief in Opposition 6, Complaint ¶19. (Footnote 2) When E. F. was five years old, her parents—petitioners Stacy and Brent Fry—obtained a trained service dog for her, as recommended by her pediatrician. The dog, a goldendoodle named Wonder, "help[s E.F.] to live as independently as possible" by assisting her with various life activities. Id., at 2, ¶3. In particular, Wonder aids E. F. by "retrieving dropped items, helping her balance when she uses her walker, opening and closing doors, turning on and off lights, helping her take off her coat, [and] helping her transfer to and from the toilet." Id., at 7, ¶27.

But when the Frys sought permission for Wonder to join E. F. in kindergarten, officials at Ezra Eby Elementary School refused the request. Under E. F.'s existing IEP, a human aide provided E.F. with one-on-one support throughout the day; that two-legged assistance, the school officials thought, rendered Wonder superfluous. In the words of one administrator, Wonder should be barred from Ezra Eby because all of E. F.'s "physical and academic needs [were] being met through the services/programs/ accommodations" that the school had already agreed to. *Id.*, at 8, ¶33. Later that year, the school officials briefly allowed Wonder to accompany E. F. to school on a trial basis; but even then, "the dog was required to remain in the back of the room during classes, and was forbidden from assisting [E. F.] with many tasks he had been specifically trained to do." *Ibid.*, ¶35. And when the trial period concluded, the administrators again informed the Frys that Wonder was not welcome. As a result, the Frys removed E. F. from Ezra Eby and began homeschooling her.

In addition, the Frys filed a complaint with the U. S. Department of Education's Office for Civil Rights (OCR), charging that Ezra Eby's exclusion of E. F.'s service animal violated her rights under Title II of the ADA and §504 of the Rehabilitation Act. Following an investigation, OCR agreed. The office explained in its decision letter that a school's obligations under those statutes go beyond providing educational services: A school could offer a FAPE to a child with a disability but still run afoul of the laws' ban on discrimination. See App. 30–32. And here, OCR found, Ezra Eby had indeed violated that ban, even if its use of a human aide satisfied the FAPE standard. See *Id.*, at 35–36. OCR analogized the school's conduct to "requir[ing] a student who uses a wheelchair to be carried" by an aide or "requir[ing] a blind student to be led [around by a] teacher" instead of permitting him to use a guide dog or cane. *Id.*, at 35. Regardless whether those—or Ezra Eby's—policies denied a FAPE, they violated Title II and §504 by discriminating against children with disabilities. See *Id.*, at 35–36.

In response to OCR's decision, school officials at last agreed that E. F. could come to school with Wonder. But after meeting with Ezra Eby's principal, the Frys became concerned that the school administration "would resent [E. F.] and make her return to school difficult." App. to Brief in Opposition 10, ¶48. Accordingly, the Frys found a different public school, in a different district, where administrators and teachers enthusiastically received both E. F. and Wonder.

C

The Frys then filed this suit in federal court against the local and regional school districts in which Ezra Eby is located, along with the school's principal (collectively, the school districts). The complaint alleged that the school districts violated Title II of the ADA and §504 of the Rehabilitation Act by "denying [E. F.] equal access" to Ezra Eby and its programs, "refus[ing] to reasonably accommodate" E. F.'s use of a service animal, and otherwise "dis- criminat[ing] against [E. F.] as a person with disabilities." *Id.*, at 15, ¶68, 17–18, ¶¶82–83. According to the com- plaint, E. F. suffered harm as a result of that discrimination, including "emotional distress and pain, embarrassment, [and] mental anguish." *Id.*, at 11–12, ¶51. In their prayer for relief, the Frys sought a declaration that the school districts had violated Title II and §504, along with money damages to compensate for E. F.'s injuries.

The District Court granted the school districts' motion to dismiss the suit, holding that §1415(l) required the Frys to first exhaust the IDEA's administrative procedures. See App. to Pet. for Cert. 50. A divided panel of the Court of Appeals for the Sixth Circuit affirmed on the same ground. In that court's view, §1415(l) applies if "the injuries [alleged in a suit] relate to the specific substantive protections of the IDEA." 788 F. 3d 622, 625 (2015). And that means, the court continued, that exhaustion is necessary whenever "the genesis and the manifestations" of the complained-of harms were "educational" in nature. *Id.*, at 627 (quoting *Charlie F. v. Board of Ed. of Skokie School Dist. 68*, 98 F. 3d 989, 993 (CA7 1996)). On that under- standing of §1415(l), the Sixth Circuit held, the Frys' suit could not proceed: Because the harms to E. F. were generally "educational"—most notably, the court reasoned, because "Wonder's absence hurt her sense of independence and social confidence at school"—the Frys had to exhaust the IDEA's procedures. 788 F. 3d, at 627. Judge Daughtrey dissented, emphasizing that in bringing their Title II and §504 claims, the Frys "did not allege the denial of a FAPE" or "seek to modify [E. F.'s] IEP in any way." *Id.*, at 634.

We granted certiorari to address confusion in the courts of appeals as to the scope of §1415(l)'s exhaustion requirement. 579 U. S. ___ (2016). (Footnote 3) We now vacate the Sixth Circuit's decision.

II

Section 1415(l) requires that a plaintiff exhaust the IDEA's procedures before filing an action under the ADA, the Rehabilitation Act, or similar laws when (but only when) her suit "seek[s] relief that is also available" under the IDEA. We first hold that to meet that statutory standard, a suit must seek relief for the denial of a FAPE, because that is the only "relief" the IDEA makes "available." We next conclude that in determining whether a suit indeed "seeks" relief for such a denial, a court should look to the substance, or gravamen, of the plaintiff's complaint. (Footnote 4)

A

In this Court, the parties have reached substantial agreement about what "relief" the IDEA makes "available" for children with disabilities—and about how the Sixth Circuit went wrong in addressing that question. The Frys maintain that such a child can obtain remedies under the IDEA for decisions that deprive her of a FAPE, but none for those that do not. So in the Frys' view, §1415(l)'s exhaustion requirement can come into play only when a suit concerns the denial of a FAPE—and not, as the Sixth Circuit held, when it merely has some articulable connection to the education of a child with a disability. See Reply Brief 13–15. The school districts, for their part, also believe that the Sixth Circuit's exhaustion standard "goes too far" because it could mandate exhaustion when a plaintiff is "seeking relief that is not in substance available" under the IDEA. Brief for Respondents 30. And in particular, the school districts acknowledge that the IDEA makes remedies available only in suits that "directly implicate[]" a FAPE—so that only in those suits can §1415(l) apply. Tr. of Oral Arg. 46. For the reasons that follow, we agree with the parties'

shared view: The only relief that an IDEA officer can give—hence the thing a plaintiff must seek in order to trigger §1415(l)'s exhaustion rule—is relief for the denial of a FAPE.

We begin, as always, with the statutory language at issue, which (at risk of repetition) compels exhaustion when a plaintiff seeks "relief" that is "available" under the IDEA. The ordinary meaning of "relief" in the context of a lawsuit is the "redress[] or benefit" that attends a favor- able judgment. Black's Law Dictionary 1161 (5th ed. 1979). And such relief is "available," as we recently explained, when it is "accessible or may be obtained." *Ross v. Blake*, 578 U. S. ___, ___ (2016) (slip op., at 8) (quoting Webster's Third New International Dictionary 150 (1993)). So to establish the scope of §1415(l), we must identify the circumstances in which the IDEA enables a person to obtain redress (or, similarly, to access a benefit).

That inquiry immediately reveals the primacy of a FAPE in the statutory scheme. In its first section, the IDEA declares as its first purpose "to ensure that all children with disabilities have available to them a free appropriate public education." §1400(d)(1)(A). That prin-cipal purpose then becomes the Act's principal command: A State receiving federal funding under the IDEA must make such an education "available to all children with disabilities." §1412(a)(1)(A). The guarantee of a FAPE to those children gives rise to the bulk of the statute's more specific provisions. For example, the IEP—"the center- piece of the statute's education delivery system"—serves as the "vehicle" or "means" of providing a FAPE. *Honig*, 484 U. S., at 311; *Rowley*, 458 U. S., at 181; see *supra*, at 2. And finally, as all the above suggests, the FAPE requirement provides the yardstick for measuring the adequacy of the education that a school offers to a child with a disability: Under that standard, this Court has held, a child is entitled to "meaningful" access to education based on her individual needs. *Rowley*, 458 U. S., at 192. (Footnote 5)

The IDEA's administrative procedures test whether a school has met that obligation—and so center on the Act's FAPE requirement. As noted earlier, any decision by a hearing officer on a request for substantive relief "shall" be "based on a determination of whether the child received a free appropriate public education." §1415(f)(3)(E)(i); see *supra*, at 3. (Footnote 6) Or said in Latin: In the IDEA's administrative process, a FAPE denial is the sine qua non. Suppose that a parent's complaint protests a school's failure to provide some accommodation for a child with a disability. If that accommodation is needed to fulfill the IDEA's FAPE requirement, the hearing officer must order relief. But if it is not, he cannot—even though the dispute is between a child with a disability and the school she at- tends. There might be good reasons, unrelated to a FAPE, for the school to make the requested accommodation. Indeed, another federal law (like the ADA or Rehabilitation Act) might require the accommodation on one of those alternative grounds. See infra, at 15. But still, the hearing officer cannot provide the requested relief. His role, under the IDEA, is to enforce the child's "substantive right" to a FAPE. Smith, 468 U. S., at 1010. And that is all. (Footnote 7)

For that reason, §1415(l)'s exhaustion rule hinges on whether a lawsuit seeks relief for the denial of a free appropriate public education. If a lawsuit charges such a denial, the plaintiff cannot escape §1415(l) merely by bringing her suit under a statute other than the IDEA—as when, for example, the plaintiffs in *Smith* claimed that a school's failure to provide a FAPE also violated the Rehabilitation Act. (Footnote 8) Rather, that plaintiff must first submit her case to an IDEA hearing officer, experienced in addressing exactly the issues she raises. But if, in a suit brought under a different statute, the remedy sought is not for the denial of a FAPE, then exhaustion of the IDEA's procedures is not required. After all, the plaintiff could not get any relief from those procedures: A hearing officer, as just explained, would have to send her away empty-handed. And that is true even when the suit arises directly from a school's treatment of a child with a disability—and so could be said to relate in some way to her education. A school's conduct toward such a child—say, some refusal to make an accommodation—might injure her in ways unrelated to a FAPE, which are addressed in statutes other than the IDEA. A complaint seeking redress for those other harms, independent of any FAPE denial, is not subject to §1415(l)'s exhaustion rule because, once again, the only "relief" the IDEA makes "available" is relief for the denial of a FAPE.

B

Still, an important question remains: How is a court to tell when a plaintiff "seeks" relief for the denial of a FAPE and when she does not? Here, too, the parties have found some common ground: By looking, they both say, to the "substance" of, rather than the labels used in, the plaintiff 's complaint. Brief for Respondents 20; Reply Brief 7–8. And here, too, we agree with that view: What matters is the crux—or, in legal-speak, the gravamen—of the plaintiff 's complaint, setting aside any attempts at artful pleading.

That inquiry makes central the plaintiff's own claims, as §1415(l) explicitly requires. The statutory language asks whether a lawsuit in fact "seeks" relief available under the IDEA—not, as a stricter exhaustion statute might, whether the suit "could have sought" relief available under the IDEA (or, what is much the same, whether any remedies "are" available under that law). See Brief for United States as Amicus Curiae 20 (contrasting §1415(l) with the exhaustion provision in the Prison Litigation Reform Act, 42 U. S. C. §1997e(a)). In effect, §1415(l) treats the plaintiff as "the master of the claim": She identifies its remedial basis—and is subject to exhaustion or not based on that choice. *Caterpillar Inc. v. Williams*, 482 U. S. 386, 392, and n. 7 (1987). A court deciding whether §1415(l) applies must therefore examine whether a plaintiff 's complaint—the principal instrument by which she describes her case—seeks relief for the denial of an appropriate education.

But that examination should consider substance, not surface. The use (or non-use) of particular labels and terms is not what matters. The inquiry, for example, does not ride on whether a complaint includes (or, alternatively, omits) the precise words(?) "FAPE" or "IEP." After all,

§1415(l)'s premise is that the plaintiff is suing under a statute other than the IDEA, like the Rehabilitation Act; in such a suit, the plaintiff might see no need to use the IDEA's distinctive language—even if she is in essence contesting the adequacy of a special education program. And still more critically, a "magic words" approach would make §1415(l)'s exhaustion rule too easy to bypass. Just last Term, a similar worry led us to hold that a court's jurisdiction under the Foreign Sovereign Immunities Act turns on the "gravamen," or "essentials," of the plaintiff's suit. *OBB Personenverkehr AG v. Sachs*, 577 U. S. ___, ___, ___, ___ (2015) (slip op., at 6, 8, 9). "[A]ny other approach," we explained, "would allow plaintiffs to evade the Act's restrictions through artful pleading." *Id.*, at ___ (slip op., at 8). So too here. Section 1415(l) is not merely a pleading hurdle. It requires exhaustion when the gravamen of a complaint seeks redress for a school's failure to provide a FAPE, even if not phrased or framed in precisely that way.

In addressing whether a complaint fits that description, a court should attend to the diverse means and ends of the statutes covering persons with disabilities—the IDEA on the one hand, the ADA and Rehabilitation Act (most notably) on the other. The IDEA, of course, protects only "children" (well, really, adolescents too) and concerns only their schooling. §1412(a)(1)(A). And as earlier noted, the statute's goal is to provide each child with meaningful access to education by offering individualized instruction and related services appropriate to her "unique needs." §1401(29); see *Rowley*, 458 U. S., at 192, 198; *supra*, at 11. By contrast, Title II of the ADA and §504 of the Rehabilitation Act cover people with disabilities of all ages, and do so both inside and outside schools. And those statutes aim to root out disability-based discrimination, enabling each covered person (sometimes by means of reasonable accommodations) to participate equally to all others in public facilities and federally funded programs. See *supra*, at 3–4. In short, the IDEA guarantees individually tailored educational services, while Title II and §504 promise non-discriminatory access to public institutions. That is not to deny some overlap in coverage: The same conduct might violate all three statutes—which is why, as in *Smith*, a plaintiff might seek relief for the denial of a FAPE under Title II and §504 as well as the IDEA. But still, the statutory differences just discussed mean that a complaint brought under Title II and §504 might instead seek relief for simple discrimination, irrespective of the IDEA's FAPE obligation.

One clue to whether the gravamen of a complaint against a school concerns the denial of a FAPE, or instead addresses disability-based discrimination, can come from asking a pair of hypothetical questions. First, could the plaintiff have brought essentially the same claim if the alleged conduct had occurred at a public facility that was not a school—say, a public theater or library? And second, could an adult at the school—say, an employee or visitor— have pressed essentially the same grievance? When the answer to those questions is yes, a complaint that does not expressly allege the denial of a FAPE is also unlikely to be truly about that subject; after all, in those other situations there is no FAPE obligation and yet the same basic suit could go forward. But when the answer is no, then the complaint probably does concern a FAPE, even if it does not explicitly say so; for the FAPE requirement is all that explains why only a child in the school setting (not an adult in that setting or a child in some other) has a viable claim.

Take two contrasting examples. Suppose first that a wheelchair-bound child sues his school for discrimination under Title II (again, without mentioning the denial of a FAPE) because the building lacks access ramps. In some sense, that architectural feature has educational consequences, and a different lawsuit might have alleged that it violates the IDEA: After all, if the child cannot get inside the school, he cannot receive instruction there; and if he must be carried inside, he may not achieve the sense of independence conducive to academic (or later to real-world) success. But is the denial of a FAPE really the gravamen of the plaintiff's Title II complaint? Consider that the child could file the same basic complaint if a municipal library or theater had no ramps. And similarly, an employee or visitor could bring a mostly identical com- plaint against the school. That the claim can stay the same in those alternative scenarios suggests that its essence is equality of access to public facilities, not adequacy of special education. See *supra*, at 7 (describing OCR's use of a similar example). And so §1415(l) does not require exhaustion. (Footnote 9)

But suppose next that a student with a learning disability sues his school under Title II for failing to provide remedial tutoring in mathematics. That suit, too, might be cast as one for disability-based discrimination, grounded on the school's refusal to make a reasonable accommodation; the complaint might make no reference at all to a FAPE or an IEP. But can anyone imagine the student making the same claim against a public theater or library? Or, similarly, imagine an adult visitor or employee suing the school to obtain a math tutorial? The difficulty of transplanting the complaint to those other contexts sug- gests that its essence—even though not its wording—is the provision of a FAPE, thus bringing §1415(l) into play. (Footnote 10)

A further sign that the gravamen of a suit is the denial of a FAPE can emerge from the history of the proceedings. In particular, a court may consider that a plaintiff has previously invoked the IDEA's formal procedures to handle the dispute—thus starting to exhaust the Act's remedies before switching midstream. Recall that a parent dissatisfied with her child's education initiates those administrative procedures by filing a complaint, which triggers a preliminary meeting (or possibly mediation) and then a due process hearing. See *supra*, at 2–3. A plaintiff 's initial choice to pursue that process may suggest that she is indeed seeking relief for the denial of a FAPE—with the shift to judicial proceedings prior to full exhaustion reflecting only strategic calculations about how to maximize the prospects of such a remedy. Whether that is so depends on the facts; a court may conclude, for example, that the move to a courtroom came from a late-acquired awareness

that the school had fulfilled its FAPE obligation and that the grievance involves something else entirely. But prior pursuit of the IDEA's administrative remedies will often provide strong evidence that the substance of a plaintiff 's claim concerns the denial of a FAPE, even if the complaint never explicitly uses that term. (Footnote 11)

III

The Court of Appeals did not undertake the analysis we have just set forward. As noted above, it asked whether E. F.'s injuries were, broadly speaking, "educational" in nature. See *supra*, at 8; 788 F. 3d, at 627 (reasoning that the "value of allowing Wonder to attend [school] with E. F. was educational" because it would foster "her sense of independence and social confidence," which is "the sort of interest the IDEA protects"). That is not the same as asking whether the gravamen of E. F.'s complaint charges, and seeks relief for, the denial of a FAPE. And that difference in standard may have led to a difference in result in this case. Understood correctly, §1415(l) might not re- quire exhaustion of the Frys' claim. We lack some important information on that score, however, and so we remand the issue to the court below.

The Frys' complaint alleges only disability-based discrimination, without making any reference to the adequacy of the special education services E. F.'s school provided. The school districts' "refusal to allow Wonder to act as a service dog," the complaint states, "discriminated against [E. F.] as a person with disabilities ... by denying her equal access" to public facilities. App. to Brief in Opposition 15, Complaint ¶68. The complaint contains no allegation about the denial of a FAPE or about any deficiency in E. F.'s IEP. More, it does not accuse the school even in general terms of refusing to provide the educational instruction and services that E. F. needs. See 788 F. 3d, at 631 (acknowledging that the Frys do not "state that Won- der enhances E. F.'s educational opportunities"). As the Frys explained in this Court: The school districts "have said all along that because they gave [E. F.] a one-on-one [human] aide, that all of her ... educational needs were satisfied. And we have not challenged that, and it would be difficult for us to challenge that." Tr. of Oral Arg. 16. The Frys instead maintained, just as OCR had earlier found, that the school districts infringed E. F.'s right to equal access—even if their actions complied in full with the IDEA's requirements. See App. to Brief in Opposition 15, 18–19, Complaint ¶¶ 69, 85, 87; App. 34–37; *supra*, at 7–8.

And nothing in the nature of the Frys' suit suggests any implicit focus on the adequacy of E. F.'s education. Con- sider, as suggested above, that the Frys could have filed essentially the same complaint if a public library or theater had refused admittance to Wonder. See *supra*, at 16. Or similarly, consider that an adult visitor to the school could have leveled much the same charges if prevented from entering with his service dog. See *ibid.* In each case, the plaintiff would challenge a public facility's policy of precluding service dogs (just as a blind person might challenge a policy of barring guide dogs, see *supra*, at 7) as violating Title II's and §504's equal access requirements. The suit would have nothing to do with the provision of educational services. From all that we know now, that is exactly the kind of action the Frys have brought.

But we do not foreclose the possibility that the history of these proceedings might suggest something different. As earlier discussed, a plaintiff 's initial pursuit of the IDEA's administrative remedies can serve as evidence that the gravamen of her later suit is the denial of a FAPE, even though that does not appear on the face of her complaint. See *supra*, at 17–18. The Frys may or may not have sought those remedies before filing this case: None of the parties here have addressed that issue, and the record is cloudy as to the relevant facts. Accordingly, on remand, the court below should establish whether (or to what extent) the Frys invoked the IDEA's dispute resolution process before bringing this suit. And if the Frys started down that road, the court should decide whether their actions reveal that the gravamen of their complaint is indeed the denial of a FAPE, thus necessitating further exhaustion.

With these instructions and for the reasons stated, we vacate the judgment of the Court of Appeals and remand the case for further proceedings consistent with this opinion.

It is so ordered.

CONCURRING OPINION

JUSTICE ALITO, with whom JUSTICE THOMAS joins, concurring in part and concurring in the judgment.

I join all of the opinion of the Court with the exception of its discussion (in the text from the beginning of the first new paragraph on page 15 to the end of the opinion) in which the Court provides several misleading "clue[s]," ante, at 15, for the lower courts.

The Court first instructs the lower courts to inquire whether the plaintiff could have brought "essentially the same claim if the alleged conduct had occurred at a public facility that was not a school—say, a public theater or library." *Ibid.* Next, the Court says, a court should ask whether "an adult at the school—say, an employee or visitor—[could] have pressed essentially the same grievance." *Ibid.* These clues make sense only if there is no overlap between the relief available under the following two sets of claims: (1) the relief provided by the Individuals with Disabilities Education Act (IDEA), and (2) the relief provided by other federal laws (including the Constitution, the Americans with Disabilities Act of 1990 (ADA), and the Rehabilitation Act of 1973). The Court does not show or even claim that there is no such overlap—to the contrary, it observes that "[t]he same conduct might violate" the ADA, the Rehabilitation Act and the IDEA. *Ibid.* And since these clues work only in the absence of overlap, I would not suggest them.

The Court provides another false clue by suggesting that lower courts take into account whether parents, before filing suit under the ADA or the Rehabilitation Act, began to pursue but then abandoned the IDEA's formal procedures. Ante, at 17–18. This clue also seems to me to be ill-advised. It is easy to imagine circumstances under which parents might start down the IDEA road and then change course and file an action under the ADA or the Rehabilitation Act that seeks relief that the IDEA cannot provide. The parents might be advised by their attorney that the relief they were seeking under the IDEA is not available under that law but is available under another. Or the parents might change their minds about the relief that they want, give up on the relief that the IDEA can provide, and turn to another statute.

Although the Court provides these clues for the purpose of assisting the lower courts, I am afraid that they may have the opposite effect. They are likely to confuse and lead courts astray.

Footnotes

[1] At the time (and until 1990), the IDEA was called the Education of the Handicapped Act, or EHA. See §901(a), 104 Stat. 1141–1142 (renaming the statute). To avoid confusion—and acronym overload— we refer throughout this opinion only to the IDEA.

[2] Because this case comes to us on review of a motion to dismiss E. F.'s suit, we accept as true all facts pleaded in her complaint. See *Leatherman v. Tarrant County Narcotics Intelligence and Coordination Unit,* 507 U. S. 163, 164 (1993).

[3] See *Payne v. Peninsula School Dist.,* 653 F. 3d 863, 874 (CA9 2011) (en banc) (cataloguing different Circuits' understandings of §1415(l)). In particular, the Ninth Circuit has criticized an approach similar to the Sixth Circuit's for "treat[ing] §1415(l) as a quasi-preemption provision, requiring administrative exhaustion for any case that falls within the general 'field' of educating disabled students." *Id.,* at 875.

[4] In reaching these conclusions, we leave for another day a further question about the meaning of §1415(l): Is exhaustion required when the plaintiff complains of the denial of a FAPE, but the specific remedy she requests—here, money damages for emotional distress—is not one that an IDEA hearing officer may award? The Frys, along

with the Solicitor General, say the answer is no. See Reply Brief 2–3; Brief for United States as Amicus Curiae 16. But resolution of that question might not be needed in this case because the Frys also say that their complaint is not about the denial of a FAPE, see Reply Brief 17—and, as later explained, we must remand that distinct issue to the Sixth Circuit, see infra, at 18–20. Only if that court rejects the Frys' view of their lawsuit, using the analysis we set out below, will the question about the effect of their request for money damages arise.

[5] A case now before this Court, *Endrew F. v. Douglas County School Dist. RE-1,* No. 15–827, presents unresolved questions about the precise content of the FAPE standard.

[6] Without finding the denial of a FAPE, a hearing officer may do nothing more than order a school district to comply with the Act's various procedural requirements, see §1415(f)(3)(E)(iii)—for example, by allowing parents to "examine all records" relating to their child, §1415(b)(1).

[7] Similarly, a court in IDEA litigation may provide a substantive remedy only when it determines that a school has denied a FAPE. See *School Comm. of Burlington v. Department of Ed. of Mass.,* 471 U. S. 359, 369 (1985). Without such a finding, that kind of relief is (once again) unavailable under the Act.

[8] Once again, we do not address here (or anywhere else in this opinion) a case in which a plaintiff, although charging the denial of a FAPE, seeks a form of remedy that an IDEA officer cannot give—for example, as in the Frys' complaint, money damages for resulting emotional injury. See n. 4, *supra.*

[9] The school districts offer another example illustrating the point. They suppose that a teacher, acting out of animus or frustration, strikes a student with a disability, who then sues the school under a statute other than the IDEA. See Brief for Respondents 36–37. Here too, the suit could be said to relate, in both genesis and effect, to the child's

education. But the school districts opine, we think correctly, that the substance of the plaintiff's claim is unlikely to involve the adequacy of special education—and thus is unlikely to require exhaustion. See *ibid.* A telling indicator of that conclusion is that a child could file the same kind of suit against an official at another public facility for inflicting such physical abuse—as could an adult subject to similar treatment by a school official. To be sure, the particular circumstances of such a suit (school or theater? student or employee?) might be pertinent in assessing the reasonableness of the challenged conduct. But even if that is so, the plausibility of bringing other variants of the suit indicates that the gravamen of the plaintiff's complaint does not concern the appropriateness of an educational program.

[10] According to JUSTICE ALITO, the hypothetical inquiries described above are useful only if the IDEA and other federal laws are mutually exclusive in scope. See post, at 1 (opinion concurring in part and concurring in judgment).

That is incorrect. The point of the questions is not to show that a plaintiff faced with a particular set of circumstances could only have proceeded under Title II or §504—or, alternatively, could only have proceeded under the IDEA. (Depending on the circumstances, she might well have been able to proceed under both.) Rather, these questions help determine whether a plaintiff who has chosen to bring a claim under Title II or §504 instead of the IDEA—and whose complaint makes no mention of a FAPE—nevertheless raises a claim whose substance is the denial of an appropriate education.

[11] The point here is limited to commencement of the IDEA's formal administrative procedures; it does not apply to more informal requests to IEP Team members or other school administrators for accommodations or changes to a special education program. After all, parents of a child with a disability are likely to bring all grievances first to those familiar officials, whether or not they involve the denial of a FAPE.

END OF *FRY* OPINION

SYLLABUS in *Fry*

[A syllabus (headnote) constitutes no part of the opinion of the Court but has been prepared by the Reporter of Decisions for the convenience of the reader. The syllabus references page numbers at the end of some paragraphs. Those page numbers reference the adobe.pdf version of this case that is available for download.]

The Individuals with Disabilities Education Act (IDEA) offers federal funds to States in exchange for a commitment to furnish a "free appropriate public education" (FAPE) to children with certain disabilities, 20 U. S. C. §1412(a)(1)(A), and establishes formal administrative procedures for resolving disputes between parents and schools concerning the provision of a FAPE. Other federal statutes also protect the interests of children with disabilities, including Title II of the Americans with Disabilities Act (ADA) and §504 of the Rehabilitation Act. In *Smith v. Robinson*, 468 U. S. 992, this Court considered the interaction between those other laws and the IDEA, holding that the IDEA was "the exclusive avenue" through which a child with a disability could challenge the adequacy of his education. *Id.*, at 1009. Congress responded by passing the Handicapped Children's Protection Act of 1986, overturning Smith's preclusion of non-IDEA claims and adding a carefully defined exhaustion provision. Under that provision, a plaintiff bringing suit under the ADA, the Rehabilitation Act, or similar laws "seeking relief that is also available under [the IDEA]" must first exhaust the IDEA's administrative procedures. §1415(l).

Petitioner E. F. is a child with a severe form of cerebral palsy; a trained service dog named Wonder assists her with various daily life activities. When E. F.'s parents, petitioners Stacy and Brent Fry, sought permission for Wonder to join E. F. in kindergarten, officials at Ezra Eby Elementary School refused. The officials reasoned that the human aide provided as part of E. F.'s individualized education program rendered the dog superfluous. In response, the Frys removed E.

F. from Ezra Eby and began homeschooling her. They also filed a complaint with the Department of Education's Office for Civil Rights (OCR), claiming that the exclusion of E. F.'s service animal violated her rights under Title II and §504. OCR agreed, and school officials invited E. F. to return to Ezra Eby with Wonder. But the Frys, concerned about resentment from school officials, instead enrolled E. F. in a different school that welcomed the service dog. The Frys then filed this suit in federal court against Ezra Eby's local and regional school districts and principal (collectively, the school districts), alleging that they violated Title II and §504 and seeking declaratory and monetary relief. The District Court granted the school districts' motion to dismiss the suit, holding that §1415(l) required the Frys to first exhaust the IDEA's administrative procedures. The Sixth Circuit affirmed, reasoning that §1415(l) applies whenever a plaintiff's alleged harms are "educational" in nature.

Held:

1. Exhaustion of the IDEA's administrative procedures is unnecessary where the gravamen of the plaintiff's suit is something other than the denial of the IDEA's core guarantee of a FAPE. Pp. 9–18.

(a) The language of §1415(l) compels exhaustion when a plaintiff seeks "relief" that is "available" under the IDEA. Establishing the scope of §1415(l), then, requires identifying the circumstances in which the IDEA enables a person to obtain redress or access a benefit. That inquiry immediately reveals the primacy of a FAPE in the statutory scheme. The IDEA's stated purpose and specific commands center on ensuring a FAPE for children with disabilities. And the IDEA's administrative procedures test whether a school has met this obligation: Any decision by a hearing officer on a request for substantive relief "shall" be "based on a determination of whether the child received a free appropriate public education."

§1415(f)(3)(E)(i). Accordingly, §1415(l)'s exhaustion rule hinges on whether a lawsuit seeks relief for the denial of a FAPE. If a lawsuit charges such a denial, the plaintiff cannot escape §1415(l) merely by bringing the suit under a statute other than the IDEA. But if the remedy sought in a suit brought under a different statute is not for the denial of a FAPE, then exhaustion of the IDEA's procedures is not required. Pp. 9–13.

(b) In determining whether a plaintiff seeks relief for the denial of a FAPE, what matters is the gravamen of the plaintiff's complaint, setting aside any attempts at artful pleading. That inquiry makes central the plaintiff's own claims, as §1415(l) explicitly requires in asking whether a lawsuit in fact "seeks" relief available under the IDEA. But examination of a plaintiff's complaint should consider substance, not surface: §1415(l) requires exhaustion when the gravamen of a complaint seeks redress for a school's failure to provide a FAPE, even if not phrased or framed in precisely that way. In addressing whether a complaint fits that description, a court should attend to the diverse means and ends of the statutes covering persons with disabilities. The IDEA guarantees individually tailored educational services for children with disabilities, while Title II and §504 promise nondiscriminatory access to public institutions for people with disabilities of all ages. That is not to deny some overlap in coverage: The same conduct might violate all three statutes. But still, these statutory differences mean that a complaint brought under Title II and §504 might instead seek relief for simple discrimination, irrespective of the IDEA's FAPE obligation. One clue to the gravamen of a complaint can come from asking a pair of hypothetical questions. First, could the plaintiff have brought essentially the same claim if the alleged conduct had occurred at a public facility that was not a school? Second, could an adult at the school have pressed essentially the same grievance? When the answer to those questions is yes, a complaint that does not expressly allege the denial of a FAPE is also unlikely to be truly about that subject. But when the answer is no, then the complaint probably does concern a FAPE. A further sign of the gravamen of a suit can emerge from the history of the proceedings. Prior pursuit of the IDEA's administrative remedies may provide strong evidence that the substance of a plaintiff's claim concerns the denial of a FAPE, even if the complaint never explicitly uses that term. Pp. 13–18.

2. This case is remanded to the Court of Appeals for a proper analysis of whether the gravamen of E. F.'s complaint charges, and seeks relief for, the denial of a FAPE. The Frys' complaint alleges only disability-based discrimination, without making any reference to the adequacy of the special education services E. F.'s school provided. Instead, the Frys have maintained that the school districts infringed E. F.'s right to equal access—even if their actions complied in full with the IDEA's requirements. But the possibility remains that the history of these proceedings might suggest something different. The parties have not addressed whether the Frys initially pursued the IDEA's administrative remedies, and the record is cloudy as to the relevant facts. On remand, the court below should establish whether (or to what extent) the Frys invoked the IDEA's dispute resolution process before filing suit. And if the Frys started down that road, the court should decide whether their actions reveal that the gravamen of their complaint is indeed the denial of a FAPE, thus necessitating further exhaustion. Pp. 18–20. 788 F. 3d 622, vacated and remanded.

END OF *FRY* SYLLABUS

Transcript of Announcement of the *Fry* Opinion by Justice Elena Kagan
February 22, 2017

"A federal statute called the Individuals with Disabilities Education Act of IDEA requires states to offer special education services to children with disabilities.

"Because parents and schools often disagree about the services that law requires, it sets up a dispute resolution mechanism, administrative procedures that have to be given a chance to work before a parent can bring suit.

"Separate and apart from the IDEA, other federal laws protect all disabled people from discrimination, including children, and guarantee them equal access to public facilities.

"Now, I am just going to call those statues 'disability discrimination laws' so we do not have too many acronyms floating around here.

"Petitioners Stacy and Brent Fry have a daughter, she is called E.F., and E.F. has a disability, a form of cerebral palsy.

"Because she needs assistance with various tasks, E.F. has a service dog named Wonder. E.F. and her parents wanted Wonder to go to school with E.F. so he could help her in all the ways he typically does.

"But the school said Wonder was not allowed.

"That instead, teachers could help E.F. with everything she needed.

"The Frys sued the school under the disability discrimination laws I mentioned, not under the IDEA.

"The question here is whether, even so, the Frys first had to go through the administrative process that the IDEA sets up.

"Or to use the legal term, whether they had to exhaust the IDEA's process.

"That question is addressed in a particular provision of the IDEA, the Exhaustion Provision.

"It says that nothing in the IDEA prevents people like the Frys from suing under discrimination laws.

"But it also says that sometimes people who want to use those laws have to first go through the IDEA's administrative process.

"When is that?

"The statute says, 'When a person is seeking relief that is also available under the IDEA.'

"This case boils down to what that phrase means.

"So, what kind of relief is available under the IDEA?

"The core requirement is something called 'a free appropriate public education.'

"That is what every state has to give to children with disabilities.

"And the only kind of relief available under the IDEA is relief for the denial of a free appropriate public education.

"You cannot get relief for anything else.

"That means whether people like the Frys have to exhaust the IDEA's administrative process turns on whether they are seeking relief for the denial of a free appropriate public education.

"If they are, then they have to exhaust the IDEA's process even though they are bringing their suit under an anti-discrimination law.

"But if they are alleging something else, not anything to do with special education but just with the denial of equal access to public facilities, then they do not have to exhaust.

"Now, that raises some questions about how you tell the difference between the two.

"It is not always about the words people like the Frys use in their complaints.

"We want to know about the substance of their claims, not a bunch of labels.

"So how do you tell what the real substance of the claim is?

"One way is to ask a couple of hypothetical questions.

"First, could the trial have brought much the same claim if the conduct had occurred at a public facility that was not a school, say, a library?

"If the answer is yes, it suggests the suit is not about special education really, it is more about discrimination and denial of access.

"And second, could and adult, say a parent, sue the school for much the same thing?

"If yes, that also suggests the claim is not really about special education.

"But when the answer to those questions is no, the suit probably is about the adequacy of educational services, and then you have to go through the IDEA's administrative process.

"Another factor we say to consider is the history of the dispute between the school and parents, if the parents started the road of IDEA's administrative process before suing, that can be strong evidence that the substance of the complaint is really about the denial of a special education.

"The Court of Appeals here did not do that analysis, so we vacate that court's decision and send the case back for further consideration of the Frys' complaint.

"Justice Alito has filed an opinion concurring in part and concurring in the judgment in which Justice Thomas joins."

END OF *FRY* TRANSCRIPT

(Wrightslaw Note: Links to the briefs and the Opinion in the *Fry* case are at:
http://www.scotusblog.com/case-files/cases/fry-v-napoleon-community-schools/

Audio Links to the Oral Argument and this Announcement of the Decision are located at:
https://www.oyez.org/cases/2016/15-497)

This page intentionally left blank for your notes.

Endrew F. v. Douglas County Sch. Dist.

Endrew F., a minor, by and through his parents and next friends, Joseph F. et. al.

v.

Douglas County School District RE-1

OPINION OF THE COURT

No. 15-827 – Argued January 11, 2017 - Decided March 22, 2017

Chief Justice ROBERTS delivered the opinion for a unanimous Court.

Thirty-five years ago, this Court held that the Individuals with Disabilities Education Act establishes a substantive right to a "free appropriate public education" for certain children with disabilities. *Board of Ed. of Hendrick Hudson Central School Dist., Westchester Cty. v. Rowley*, 458 U.S. 176, 102 S.Ct. 3034, 73 L.Ed.2d 690 (1982). We declined, however, to endorse any one standard for determining "when handicapped children are receiving sufficient educational benefits to satisfy the requirements of the Act." *Id.*, at 202, 102 S.Ct. 3034. That "more difficult problem" is before us today. *Ibid.*

I

A

The Individuals with Disabilities Education Act (IDEA or Act) offers States federal funds to assist in educating children with disabilities. 84 Stat. 175, as amended, 20 U.S.C. § 1400 *et seq.*; see *Arlington Central School Dist. Bd. of Ed. v. Murphy*, 548 U.S. 291, 295, 126 S.Ct. 2455, 165 L.Ed.2d 526 (2006). In exchange for the funds, a State pledges to comply with a number of statutory conditions. Among them, the State must provide a free appropriate public education — a FAPE, for short — to all eligible children. § 1412(a)(1).

A FAPE, as the Act defines it, includes both "special education" and "related services." § 1401(9). "Special education" is "specially designed instruction ... to meet the unique needs of a child with a disability"; "related services" are the support services "required to assist a child ... to benefit from" that instruction. §§ 1401(26), (29). A State covered by the IDEA must provide a disabled child with such special education and related services "in conformity with the [child's] individualized education program," or IEP. § 1401(9)(D).

The IEP is "the centerpiece of the statute's education delivery system for disabled children." *Honig v. Doe*, 484 U.S. 305, 311, 108 S.Ct. 592, 98 L.Ed.2d 686 (1988). A comprehensive plan prepared by a child's "IEP Team" (which includes teachers, school officials, and the child's parents), an IEP must be drafted in compliance with a detailed set of procedures. § 1414(d)(1)(B) (internal quotation marks omitted). These procedures emphasize collaboration among parents and educators and require careful consideration of the child's individual circumstances. § 1414. The IEP is the means by which special education and related services are "tailored to the unique needs" of a particular child. *Rowley*, 458 U.S., at 181, 102 S.Ct. 3034.

The IDEA requires that every IEP include "a statement of the child's present levels of academic achievement and functional performance," describe "how the child's disability affects the child's involvement and progress in the general education curriculum," and set out "measurable annual goals, including academic and functional goals," along with a "description of how the child's progress toward meeting" those goals will be gauged. §§ 1414(d)(1)(A)(i)(I)-(III). The IEP must also describe the "special education and related services ... that will be provided" so that the child may "advance appropriately toward attaining the annual goals" and, when possible, "be involved in and make progress in the general education curriculum." § 1414(d)(1)(A)(i)(IV).

Parents and educators often agree about what a child's IEP should contain. But not always. When disagreement arises, parents may turn to dispute resolution procedures established by the IDEA. The parties may resolve their differences informally, through a "[p]reliminary meeting," or, somewhat more formally, through mediation. §§ 1415(e), (f)(1)(B)(i). If these measures fail to produce accord, the parties may proceed to what the Act calls a "due process hearing" before a state or local educational agency. §§ 1415(f)(1)(A), (g). And at the conclusion of the administrative process, the losing party may seek redress in state or federal court. § 1415(i)(2)(A).

B

This Court first addressed the FAPE requirement in *Rowley*. (Footnote 1) Plaintiff Amy *Rowley* was a first grader with impaired hearing. Her school district offered an IEP under which Amy would receive instruction in the regular classroom and spend time each week with a special tutor and a speech therapist. The district proposed that Amy's classroom teacher speak into a wireless transmitter and that Amy use an FM hearing aid

designed to amplify her teacher's words; the district offered to supply both components of this system. But Amy's parents argued that the IEP should go further and provide a sign-language interpreter in all of her classes. Contending that the school district's refusal to furnish an interpreter denied Amy a FAPE, Amy's parents initiated administrative proceedings, then filed a lawsuit under the Act. *Rowley*, 458 U.S., at 184-185, 102 S.Ct. 3034.

The District Court agreed that Amy had been denied a FAPE. The court acknowledged that Amy was making excellent progress in school: She was "perform[ing] better than the average child in her class" and "advancing easily from grade to grade." *Id.*, at 185, 102 S.Ct. 3034 (internal quotation marks omitted). At the same time, Amy "under[stood] considerably less of what goes on in class than she could if she were not deaf." *Ibid.* (internal quotation marks omitted). Concluding that "it has been left entirely to the courts and the hearings officers to give content to the requirement of an `appropriate education,'" 483 F.Supp. 528, 533 (S.D.N.Y. 1980), the District Court ruled that Amy's education was not "appropriate" unless it provided her "an opportunity to achieve [her] full potential commensurate with the opportunity provided to other children." *Rowley*, 458 U.S., at 185-186, 102 S.Ct. 3034 (internal quotation marks omitted). The Second Circuit agreed with this analysis and affirmed.

In this Court, the parties advanced starkly different understandings of the FAPE requirement. Amy's parents defended the approach of the lower courts, arguing that the school district was required to provide instruction and services that would provide Amy an "equal educational opportunity" relative to children without disabilities. *Id.*, at 198, 102 S.Ct. 3034 (internal quotation marks omitted). The school district, for its part, contended that the IDEA "did not create substantive individual rights"; the FAPE provision was instead merely aspirational. Brief for Petitioners in *Rowley*, O.T. 1981, No. 80-1002, pp. 28, 41.

Neither position carried the day. On the one hand, this Court rejected the view that the IDEA gives "courts carte blanche to impose upon the States whatever burden their various judgments indicate should be imposed." *Rowley*, 458 U.S., at 190, n. 11, 102 S.Ct. 3034. After all, the statutory phrase "free appropriate public education" was expressly defined in the Act, even if the definition "tend[ed] toward the cryptic rather than the comprehensive." *Id.*, at 188, 102 S.Ct. 3034. This Court went on to reject the "equal opportunity" standard adopted by the lower courts, concluding that "free appropriate public education" was a phrase "too complex to be captured by the word 'equal' whether one is speaking of opportunities or services." *Id.*, at 199, 102 S.Ct. 3034. The Court also viewed the standard as "entirely unworkable," apt to require "impossible measurements and comparisons" that courts were ill suited to make. *Id.*, at 198, 102 S.Ct. 3034.

On the other hand, the Court also rejected the school district's argument that the FAPE requirement was actually no requirement at all. *Id.*, at 200, 102 S.Ct. 3034. Instead, the Court carefully charted a middle path. Even though "Congress was rather sketchy in establishing substantive requirements" under the Act, *Id.*, at 206, 102 S.Ct. 3034 the Court nonetheless made clear that the Act guarantees a substantively adequate program of education to all eligible children, *Id.*, at 200-202, 207, 102 S.Ct. 3034; see *Id.*, at 193, n. 15, 102 S.Ct. 3034 (describing the "substantive standard ... implicit in the Act"). We explained that this requirement is satisfied, and a child has received a FAPE, if the child's IEP sets out an educational program that is "reasonably calculated to enable the child to receive educational benefits." *Id.*, at 207, 102 S.Ct. 3034. For children receiving instruction in the regular classroom, this would generally require an IEP "reasonably calculated to enable the child to achieve passing marks and advance from grade to grade." *Id.*, at 204, 102 S.Ct. 3034; see also *id.*, at 203, n. 25, 102 S.Ct. 3034.

In view of Amy *Rowley*'s excellent progress and the "substantial" suite of specialized instruction and services offered in her IEP, we concluded that her program satisfied the FAPE requirement. *Id.*, at 202, 102 S.Ct. 3034. But we went no further.

Instead, we expressly "confine[d] our analysis" to the facts of the case before us. *Ibid.* Observing that the Act requires States to "educate a wide spectrum" of children with disabilities and that "the benefits obtainable by children at one end of the spectrum will differ dramatically from those obtainable by children at the other end," we declined "to establish any one test for determining the adequacy of educational benefits conferred upon all children covered by the Act." *Ibid.*

C

Petitioner Endrew F. was diagnosed with autism at age two. Autism is a neurodevelopmental disorder generally marked by impaired social and communicative skills, "engagement in repetitive activities and stereotyped movements, resistance to environmental change or change in daily routines, and unusual responses to sensory experiences." 34 C.F.R. § 300.8(c)(1)(i) (2016); see Brief for Petitioner 8. A child with autism qualifies as a "[c]hild with a disability" under the IDEA, and Colorado (where Endrew resides) accepts IDEA funding. § 1401(3)(A). Endrew is therefore entitled to the benefits of the Act, including a FAPE provided by the State.

Endrew attended school in respondent Douglas County School District from preschool through fourth grade. Each year, his IEP Team drafted an IEP addressed to his educational and functional needs. By Endrew's fourth grade year, however, his parents had become dissatisfied with his progress. Although Endrew displayed a number of strengths — his teachers described him as a humorous child with a "sweet disposition" who "show[ed] concern[] for friends" — he still "exhibited multiple behaviors that inhibited his ability to access learning in the classroom." Supp. App. 182a; 798 F.3d 1329, 1336 (C.A.10 2015). Endrew would scream in class, climb over furniture and other students, and occasionally run away from school. *Id.*, at 1336. He was afflicted by severe fears of common-place things like flies, spills, and public restrooms. As Endrew's parents saw it, his academic and functional progress had essentially stalled: Endrew's IEPs largely carried over the same basic goals and objectives from one year to the next, indicating that he was failing to make meaningful progress toward his aims. His parents believed that only a thorough overhaul of the school district's approach to Endrew's behavioral problems could reverse the trend. But in April 2010, the school district presented Endrew's parents with a proposed fifth grade IEP that was, in their view, pretty much the same as his past ones. So his parents removed Endrew from public school and enrolled him at Firefly Autism House, a private school that specializes in educating children with autism.

Endrew did much better at Firefly. The school developed a "behavioral intervention plan" that identified Endrew's most problematic behaviors and set out particular strategies for addressing them. See Supp. App. 198a-201a. Firefly also added heft to Endrew's academic goals. Within months, Endrew's behavior improved significantly, permitting him to make a degree of academic progress that had eluded him in public school.

In November 2010, some six months after Endrew started classes at Firefly, his parents again met with representatives of the Douglas County School District. The district presented a new IEP. Endrew's parents considered the IEP no more adequate than the one proposed in April, and rejected it. They were particularly concerned that the stated plan for addressing Endrew's behavior did not differ meaningfully from the plan in his fourth grade IEP, despite the fact that his experience at Firefly suggested that he would benefit from a different approach.

In February 2012, Endrew's parents filed a complaint with the Colorado Department of Education seeking reimbursement for Endrew's tuition at Firefly. To qualify for such relief, they were required to show that the school district had not provided Endrew a FAPE in a timely manner prior to his enrollment at the private school. See § 1412(a)(10)(C)(ii). Endrew's parents contended that the final IEP proposed by the school district was not "reasonably calculated to enable [Endrew] to receive educational benefits" and that Endrew had therefore been denied a FAPE. *Rowley*, 458

U.S., at 207, 102 S.Ct. 3034. An Administrative Law Judge (ALJ) disagreed and denied relief.

Endrew's parents sought review in Federal District Court. Giving "due weight" to the decision of the ALJ, the District Court affirmed. 2014 WL 4548439, *5 (D.Colo., Sept. 15, 2014) (quoting *Rowley*, 458 U.S., at 206, 102 S.Ct. 3034). The court acknowledged that Endrew's performance under past IEPs "did not reveal immense educational growth." 2014 WL 4548439, at *9. But it concluded that annual modifications to Endrew's IEP objectives were "sufficient to show a pattern of, at the least, minimal progress." *Ibid.* Because Endrew's previous IEPs had enabled him to make this sort of progress, the court reasoned, his latest, similar IEP was reasonably calculated to do the same thing. In the court's view, that was all *Rowley* demanded. 2014 WL 4548439, at *9.

The Tenth Circuit affirmed. The Court of Appeals recited language from *Rowley* stating that the instruction and services furnished to children with disabilities must be calculated to confer "some educational benefit." 798 F.3d, at 1338 (quoting *Rowley*, 458 U.S., at 200, 102 S.Ct. 3034; emphasis added by Tenth Circuit). The court noted that it had long interpreted this language to mean that a child's IEP is adequate as long as it is calculated to confer an "educational benefit [that is] merely ... more than de minimis." 798 F.3d, at 1338 (internal quotation marks omitted). Applying this standard, the Tenth Circuit held that Endrew's IEP had been "reasonably calculated to enable [him] to make some progress." *Id.*, at 1342 (internal quotation marks omitted). Accordingly, he had not been denied a FAPE.

We granted certiorari. 579 U.S. ___, 137 S.Ct. 29, 195 L.Ed.2d 901 (2016).

II

A

The Court in *Rowley* declined "to establish any one test for determining the adequacy of educational benefits conferred upon all children covered by the Act." 458 U.S., at 202, 102 S.Ct. 3034. The school district, however, contends that

Rowley nonetheless established that "an IEP need not promise any particular level of benefit," so long as it is "'reasonably calculated' to provide some benefit, as opposed to none." Brief for Respondent 15.

The district relies on several passages from *Rowley* to make its case. It points to our observation that "any substantive standard prescribing the level of education to be accorded" children with disabilities was "[n]oticeably absent from the language of the statute." 458 U.S., at 189, 102 S.Ct. 3034; see Brief for Respondent 14. The district also emphasizes the Court's statement that the Act requires States to provide access to instruction "sufficient to confer some educational benefit," reasoning that any benefit, however minimal, satisfies this mandate. Brief for Respondent 15 (quoting *Rowley*, 458 U.S., at 200, 102 S.Ct. 3034). Finally, the district urges that the Court conclusively adopted a "some educational benefit" standard when it wrote that "the intent of the Act was more to open the door of public education to handicapped children ... than to guarantee any particular level of education." *Id.*, at 192, 102 S.Ct. 3034; see Brief for Respondent 14.

These statements in isolation do support the school district's argument. But the district makes too much of them. Our statement that the face of the IDEA imposed no explicit substantive standard must be evaluated alongside our statement that a substantive standard was "implicit in the Act." *Rowley*, 458 U.S., at 193, n. 15, 102 S.Ct. 3034. Similarly, we find little significance in the Court's language concerning the requirement that States provide instruction calculated to "confer some educational benefit." *Id.*, at 200, 102 S.Ct. 3034. The Court had no need to say anything more particular, since the case before it involved a child whose progress plainly demonstrated that her IEP was designed to deliver more than adequate educational benefits. See *id.*, at 202, 209-210, 102 S.Ct. 3034. The Court's principal concern was to correct what it viewed as the surprising rulings below: that the IDEA effectively empowers judges to elaborate a federal common law of public education, and that a child performing better than most in her class had

been denied a FAPE. The Court was not concerned with precisely articulating a governing standard for closer cases. See *id.*, at 202, 102 S.Ct. 3034. And the statement that the Act did not "guarantee any particular level of education" simply reflects the unobjectionable proposition that the IDEA cannot and does not promise "any particular [educational] outcome." *Id.*, at 192, 102 S.Ct. 3034 (internal quotation marks omitted). No law could do that — for any child.

More important, the school district's reading of these isolated statements runs headlong into several points on which *Rowley* is crystal clear. For instance — just after saying that the Act requires instruction that is "sufficient to confer some educational benefit" — we noted that "[t]he determination of when handicapped children are receiving sufficient educational benefits ... presents a ... difficult problem." *Id.*, at 200, 202, 102 S.Ct. 3034 (emphasis added). And then we expressly declined "to establish any one test for determining the adequacy of educational benefits" under the Act. *Id.*, at 202, 102 S.Ct. 3034 (emphasis added). It would not have been "difficult" for us to say when educational benefits are sufficient if we had just said that any educational benefit was enough. And it would have been strange to refuse to set out a test for the adequacy of educational benefits if we had just done exactly that. We cannot accept the school district's reading of *Rowley*.

B

While *Rowley* declined to articulate an overarching standard to evaluate the adequacy of the education provided under the Act, the decision and the statutory language point to a general approach: To meet its substantive obligation under the IDEA, a school must offer an IEP reasonably calculated to enable a child to make progress appropriate in light of the child's circumstances.

The "reasonably calculated" qualification reflects a recognition that crafting an appropriate program of education requires a prospective judgment by school officials. *Id.*, at 207, 102 S.Ct. 3034. The Act contemplates that this fact-intensive exercise will be informed not only by the expertise of school officials, but also by the input of the child's parents or guardians. *Id.*, at 208-209, 102 S.Ct. 3034. Any review of an IEP must appreciate that the question is whether the IEP is reasonable, not whether the court regards it as ideal. *Id.*, at 206-207, 102 S.Ct. 3034.

The IEP must aim to enable the child to make progress. After all, the essential function of an IEP is to set out a plan for pursuing academic and functional advancement. See §§ 1414(d)(1)(A)(i)(I)-(IV). This reflects the broad purpose of the IDEA, an "ambitious" piece of legislation enacted "in response to Congress' perception that a majority of handicapped children in the United States 'were either totally excluded from school or [were] sitting idly in regular classrooms awaiting the time when they were old enough to "drop out."'" *Rowley*, 458 U.S., at 179, 102 S.Ct. 3034 (quoting H.R.Rep. No. 94-332, p. 2 (1975)). A substantive standard not focused on student progress would do little to remedy the pervasive and tragic academic stagnation that prompted Congress to act.

That the progress contemplated by the IEP must be appropriate in light of the child's circumstances should come as no surprise. A focus on the particular child is at the core of the IDEA. The instruction offered must be "specially designed" to meet a child's "unique needs" through an "[i]ndividualized education program." §§ 1401(29), (14) (emphasis added). An IEP is not a form document. It is constructed only after careful consideration of the child's present levels of achievement, disability, and potential for growth. §§ 1414(d)(1)(A)(i)(I)-(IV), (d)(3)(A)(i)-(iv). As we observed in *Rowley*, the IDEA "requires participating States to educate a wide spectrum of handicapped children," and "the benefits obtainable by children at one end of the spectrum will differ dramatically from those obtainable by children at the other end, with infinite variations in between." 458 U.S., at 202, 102 S.Ct. 3034.

Rowley sheds light on what appropriate progress will look like in many cases. There, the Court recognized that the IDEA requires that children with disabilities receive education in the regular classroom "whenever possible." *Ibid.* (citing § 1412(a)(5)). When this preference is met, "the system itself monitors the educational progress of the child." *Id.*, at 202-203, 102 S.Ct. 3034. "Regular examinations are administered, grades are awarded, and yearly advancement to higher grade levels is permitted for those children who attain an adequate knowledge of the course material." *Id.*, at 203, 102 S.Ct. 3034. Progress through this system is what our society generally means by an "education." And access to an "education" is what the IDEA promises. *Ibid.* Accordingly, for a child fully integrated in the regular classroom, an IEP typically should, as *Rowley* put it, be "reasonably calculated to enable the child to achieve passing marks and advance from grade to grade." *Id.*, at 203-204, 102 S.Ct. 3034.

This guidance is grounded in the statutory definition of a FAPE. One of the components of a FAPE is "special education," defined as "specially designed instruction... to meet the unique needs of a child with a disability." §§ 1401(9), (29). In determining what it means to "meet the unique needs" of a child with a disability, the provisions governing the IEP development process are a natural source of guidance: It is through the IEP that "[t]he 'free appropriate public education' required by the Act is tailored to the unique needs of" a particular child. *Id.*, at 181, 102 S.Ct. 3034.

The IEP provisions reflect *Rowley*'s expectation that, for most children, a FAPE will involve integration in the regular classroom and individualized special education calculated to achieve advancement from grade to grade. Every IEP begins by describing a child's present level of achievement, including explaining "how the child's disability affects the child's involvement and progress in the general education curriculum." § 1414(d)(1)(A)(i)(I)(aa). It then sets out "a statement of measurable annual goals... designed to ... enable the child to be involved in and make progress in the general education curriculum," along with a description of specialized instruction and services that the child will receive. §§ 1414(d)(1)(A)(i)(II), (IV). The instruction and services must likewise be provided with an eye toward "progress in the general education curriculum." § 1414(d)(1)(A)(i)(IV)(bb). Similar IEP requirements have been in place since the time the States began accepting funding under the IDEA.

The school district protests that these provisions impose only procedural requirements — a checklist of items the IEP must address — not a substantive standard enforceable in court. Tr. of Oral Arg. 50-51. But the procedures are there for a reason, and their focus provides insight into what it means, for purposes of the FAPE definition, to "meet the unique needs" of a child with a disability. §§ 1401(9), (29). When a child is fully integrated in the regular classroom, as the Act prefers, what that typically means is providing a level of instruction reasonably calculated to permit advancement through the general curriculum. (Footnote 2)

Rowley had no need to provide concrete guidance with respect to a child who is not fully integrated in the regular classroom and not able to achieve on grade level. That case concerned a young girl who was progressing smoothly through the regular curriculum. If that is not a reasonable prospect for a child, his IEP need not aim for grade-level advancement. But his educational program must be appropriately ambitious in light of his circumstances, just as advancement from grade to grade is appropriately ambitious for most children in the regular classroom. The goals may differ, but every child should have the chance to meet challenging objectives.

Of course this describes a general standard, not a formula. But whatever else can be said about it, this standard is markedly more demanding than the "merely more than *de minimis*" test applied by the Tenth Circuit. It cannot be the case that the Act typically aims for grade-level advancement for children with disabilities who can be educated in the regular classroom, but is satisfied with barely more than *de minimis* progress for those who cannot.

When all is said and done, a student offered an educational program providing "merely more than *de minimis*" progress from year to year can hardly be said to have been offered an education at all. For children with disabilities, receiving instruction that aims so low would be tantamount to "sitting idly ... awaiting the time when they were old enough to `drop out.'" *Rowley*, 458 U.S., at 179, 102 S.Ct. 3034 (some internal quotation marks omitted). The IDEA demands more. It requires an educational program reasonably calculated to enable a child to make progress appropriate in light of the child's circumstances.

C

Endrew's parents argue that the Act goes even further. In their view, a FAPE is "an education that aims to provide a child with a disability opportunities to achieve academic success, attain self-sufficiency, and contribute to society that are substantially equal to the opportunities afforded children without disabilities." Brief for Petitioner 40.

This standard is strikingly similar to the one the lower courts adopted in *Rowley*, and it is virtually identical to the formulation advanced by Justice Blackmun in his separate writing in that case. See 458 U.S., at 185-186, 102 S.Ct. 3034; *id.*, at 211, 102 S.Ct. 3034 (opinion concurring in judgment) ("[T]he question is whether Amy's program ... offered her an opportunity to understand and participate in the classroom that was substantially equal to that given her non-handicapped classmates"). But the majority rejected any such standard in clear terms. *Id.*, at 198, 102 S.Ct. 3034 ("The requirement that States provide 'equal' educational opportunities would ... seem to present an entirely unworkable standard requiring impossible measurements and comparisons"). Mindful that Congress (despite several intervening amendments to the IDEA) has not materially changed the statutory definition of a FAPE since *Rowley* was decided, we decline to interpret the FAPE provision in a manner so plainly at odds with the Court's analysis in that case. Compare § 1401(18) (1976 ed.) with § 1401(9) (2012 ed.).

D

We will not attempt to elaborate on what "appropriate" progress will look like from case to case. It is in the nature of the Act and the standard we adopt to resist such an effort: The adequacy of a given IEP turns on the unique circumstances of the child for whom it was created. This absence of a bright-line rule, however, should not be mistaken for "an invitation to the courts to substitute their own notions of sound educational policy for those of the school authorities which they review." *Rowley*, 458 U.S., at 206, 102 S.Ct. 3034.

At the same time, deference is based on the application of expertise and the exercise of judgment by school authorities. The Act vests these officials with responsibility for decisions of critical importance to the life of a disabled child. The nature of the IEP process, from the initial consultation through state administrative proceedings, ensures that parents and school representatives will fully air their respective opinions on the degree of progress a child's IEP should pursue. See §§ 1414, 1415; *id.*, at 208-209, 102 S.Ct. 3034. By the time any dispute reaches court, school authorities will have had a complete opportunity to bring their expertise and judgment to bear on areas of disagreement. A reviewing court may fairly expect those authorities to be able to offer a cogent and responsive explanation for their decisions that shows the IEP is reasonably calculated to enable the child to make progress appropriate in light of his circumstances.

The judgment of the United States Court of Appeals for the Tenth Circuit is vacated, and the case is remanded for further proceedings consistent with this opinion.

It is so ordered.

Footnotes

[1] The requirement was initially set out in the Education of the Handicapped Act, which was later amended and renamed the IDEA. See Pub. L. 101-476, § 901(a), 104 Stat. 1141. For simplicity's sake — and to avoid "acronym overload" — we use the latter title throughout this opinion. *Fry v. Napoleon Community Schools*, 580 U.S. ___, ___, n. 1, 137 S.Ct. 743, 750, n. 1, ___ L.E.2d ___ (2017).

[2] This guidance should not be interpreted as an inflexible rule. We declined to hold in *Rowley*, and do not hold today, that "every handicapped child who is advancing from grade to grade ... is automatically receiving a [FAPE]." *Board of Ed. of Hendrick Hudson Central School Dist., Westchester Cty. v. Rowley*, 458 U.S. 176, 203, n. 25, 102 S.Ct. 3034, 73 L.Ed.2d 690 (1982).

END OF *ENDREW F.* OPINION

SYLLABUS of *Endrew F.*

[A syllabus (headnote) constitutes no part of the opinion of the Court but has been prepared by the Reporter of Decisions for the convenience of the reader. The syllabus references page numbers at the end of some paragraphs. Those page numbers reference the adobe.pdf version of this case that is available for download.]

The Individuals with Disabilities Education Act (IDEA) offers States federal funds to assist in educating children with disabilities. The Act conditions that funding on compliance with certain statutory requirements, including the requirement that States provide every eligible child a "free appropriate public education," or FAPE, by means of a uniquely tailored "individualized education program," or IEP. 20 U.S.C. §§ 1401(9)(D), 1412(a)(1).

This Court first addressed the FAPE requirement in Board of Ed. of *Hendrick Hudson Central School Dist., Westchester Cty. v. Rowley*, 458 U.S. 176, 102 S.Ct. 3034, 73 L.Ed.2d 690. The Court held that the Act guarantees a substantively adequate program of education to all eligible children, and that this requirement is satisfied if the child's IEP sets out an educational program that is "reasonably calculated to enable the child to receive educational benefits." *Id.*, at 207, 102 S.Ct. 3034. For children fully integrated in the regular classroom, this would typically require an IEP "reasonably calculated to enable the child to achieve passing marks and advance from grade to grade." *Id.*, at 204, 102 S.Ct. 3034. Because the IEP challenged in *Rowley* plainly met this standard, the Court declined "to establish any one test for determining the adequacy of educational benefits conferred upon all children covered by the Act," instead "confin[ing] its analysis" to the facts of the case before it. *Id.*, at 202, 102 S.Ct. 3034.

Petitioner Endrew F., a child with autism, received annual IEPs in respondent Douglas County School District from preschool through fourth grade. By fourth grade, Endrew's parents believed his academic and functional progress had stalled. When the school district proposed a fifth grade IEP that resembled those from past years, Endrew's parents removed him from public school and enrolled him in a specialized private school, where he made significant progress. School district representatives later presented Endrew's parents with a new fifth grade IEP, but they considered it no more adequate than the original plan. They then sought reimbursement for Endrew's private school tuition by filing a complaint under the IDEA with the Colorado Department of Education. Their claim was denied, and a Federal District Court affirmed that determination. The Tenth Circuit also affirmed. That court interpreted *Rowley* to establish a rule that a child's IEP is adequate as long as it is calculated to confer an "educational benefit [that is] merely ... more than de minimis," 798 F.3d 1329, 1338 (internal quotation marks omitted), and concluded that Endrew's IEP had been "reasonably calculated to enable [him] to make some progress," *id.*, at 1342 (internal quotation marks omitted). The court accordingly held that Endrew had received a FAPE.

Held: To meet its substantive obligation under the IDEA, a school must offer an IEP reasonably calculated to enable a child to make progress appropriate in light of the child's circumstances. Pp. 997-1002.

(a) *Rowley* and the language of the IDEA point to the approach adopted here. The "reasonably calculated" qualification reflects a recognition that crafting an appropriate program of education requires a prospective judgment by school officials, informed by their own expertise and the views of a child's parents or guardians; any review of an IEP must appreciate that the question is whether the IEP is reasonable, not whether the court regards it as ideal. An IEP must aim to enable the child to make progress; the essential function of an IEP is to set out a plan for pursuing academic and functional advancement. And the degree of progress contemplated by the IEP must be appropriate in light of the child's circumstances, which should come as no surprise. This reflects the focus on the particular child that is at the core of the IDEA, and the directive that States offer instruction "specially designed" to meet a child's "unique needs" through an "[i]ndividualized education program." §§ 1401(29), (14) (emphasis added).

Rowley sheds light on what appropriate progress will look like in many cases: For a child fully integrated in the regular classroom, an IEP typically should be "reasonably calculated to enable the child to achieve passing marks and advance from grade to grade." 458 U.S., at 204, 102 S.Ct. 3034. This guidance is grounded in the statutory definition of a FAPE. One component of a FAPE is "special education," defined as "specially designed instruction... to meet the unique needs of a child with a disability." §§ 1401(9), (29). In determining what it means to "meet the unique needs" of a child with a disability, the provisions of the IDEA governing the IEP development process provide guidance. These provisions reflect what the Court said in *Rowley* by focusing on "progress in the general education curriculum." §§ 1414(d)(1)(A)(i)(I)(aa), (II)(aa), (IV)(bb).

Rowley did not provide concrete guidance with respect to a child who is not fully integrated in the regular classroom and not able to achieve on grade level. A child's IEP need not aim for grade-level advancement if that is not a reasonable prospect. But that child's educational program must be appropriately ambitious in light of his circumstances, just as advancement from grade to grade is appropriately ambitious for most children in the regular classroom. The goals may differ, but every child should have the chance to meet challenging objectives.

This standard is more demanding than the "merely more than *de minimis*" test applied by the Tenth Circuit. It cannot be right that the IDEA generally contemplates grade-level advancement for children with disabilities who are fully integrated in the regular classroom, but is satisfied with barely more than *de minimis* progress for children who are not. Pp. 997-1001.

(b) Endrew's parents argue that the Act goes even further and requires States to provide children with disabilities educational opportunities that are "substantially equal to the opportunities afforded children without disabilities." Brief for Petitioner 40. But the lower courts in *Rowley* adopted a strikingly similar standard, and this Court rejected it in clear terms. Mindful that Congress has not materially changed the statutory definition of a FAPE since *Rowley* was decided, this Court declines to interpret the FAPE provision in a manner so plainly at odds with the Court's analysis in that case. Pp. 999-1001.

(c) The adequacy of a given IEP turns on the unique circumstances of the child for whom it was created. This absence of a bright-line rule should not be mistaken for "an invitation to the courts to substitute their own notions of sound educational policy for those of the school authorities which they review." *Rowley*, 458 U.S., at 206, 102 S.Ct. 3034. At the same time, deference is based on the application of expertise and the exercise of judgment by school authorities. The nature of the IEP process ensures that parents and school representatives will fully air their respective opinions on the degree of progress a child's IEP should pursue; thus, by the time any dispute reaches court, school authorities will have had the chance to bring their expertise and judgment to bear on areas of disagreement. See §§ 1414, 1415; *Rowley*, 458 U.S., at 208-209, 102 S.Ct. 3034. At that point, a reviewing court may fairly expect those authorities to be able to offer a cogent and responsive explanation for their decisions that shows the IEP is reasonably calculated to enable the child to make progress appropriate in light of his circumstances. Pp. 999-1002.

END OF *ENDREW F.* SYLLABUS

Transcript of Announcement of the *Endrew F.* Opinion
by Chief Justice John G. Roberts, Jr.
March 22, 2017

"I have the opinion of the Court this morning in case 15-827, *Endrew F. versus Douglas County School District.*

"The Individuals with Disabilities Education Act or the IDEA offers States federal funds to help in educating children with disabilities.

"In exchange for the money, a state agrees to comply with a long list of conditions.

"One of them is that the state must provide a 'free appropriate public education' or FAPE for short to all eligible children.

"A FAPE consists of specialized instruction tailored to a child's particular abilities and needs.

"A school sets out its instructional plan for a particular child in a document called an Individualized Education Program or IEP.

"The IEP is crafted through a collaborative process involving teachers, school officials, and the child's parents or guardians.

"Together, they prepare a comprehensive educational plan that identifies the child's needs and abilities, sets goals for the child and describes the special services the school will provide to make those goals attainable.

"Educators and parents often agree about what a child's IEP should contain, but parents sometimes determine that the IEP offered by the school is inadequate.

"Now when this happens, the parents may seek relief in court and the court must determine whether the IEP satisfies the FAPE requirement.

"Thirty-five years ago in a case called *Rowley*, we held that a child's IEP is adequate and the child has received a FAPE if the IEP is 'reasonably

calculated to enable the child to receive educational benefits'.

"The petitioner in this case Endrew F., a child, was diagnosed with autism when he was two years old.

"From preschool to fourth grade, Endrew attended school in the Douglas County School District, receiving an IEP each year.

"By the time Endrew was in fourth grade; however, his parents had become dissatisfied with his progress.

"They believed that Endrew's IEPs did not do enough to address his behavioral difficulties and as a result, were able to set only modest academic goals.

"If the school did more to address Endrew's behavior, they reasoned, it would also be able to aim for more academic progress.

"When the school proposed a fifth grade IEP that Endrew's parents considered no different than his past ones, they removed Endrew from public school and enrolled him at a private school that specializes in educating children with autism.

"Endrew's new school adopted strategies for addressing his behavior and added heft to his academic goals.

"His behavior improved and he soon made the kind of academic progress that had eluded him in the past.

"Now the IDEA entitles parents to reimbursement for private school tuition if their child did not receive a FAPE in public school.

"Endrew's parents sought reimbursement, but their claim was denied in the administrative proceeding then denied in federal district court.

"The Court of Appeals affirmed that denial.

"The Court of Appeals read our decision in *Rowley* to say that a child has received the FAPE as long as his IEP is calculated to confer 'some educational benefit'.

"The Court explained that the standard is satisfied as long as the IEP is designed to enable the child to make progress that is 'merely more than *de minimis*'.

"Our decision in *Rowley* and the text of the IDEA, however, point to a more demanding standard.

"To satisfy the FAPE requirement, a school must offer an IEP reasonably calculated to enable a child to make progress appropriate in light of the child's circumstances.

"Now, in saying that an IEP must be reasonably calculated to achieve its ends, we recognize the crafting and educational program for a child with a disability involves both the expert judgment of school officials and the input of the children's parents or guardians.

"The court reviewing an IEP must appreciate that the question is whether the IEP is reasonable not whether the court regards it as ideal.

"It is clear that an IEP must aim for progress, after all the basic function on an IEP is to set out a plan for pursuing academic and functional advancement for the child.

"A standard not focused on student progress would fail to remedy the pervasive academics stagnation experienced by disabled children that prompted Congress to act.

"Finally, the progress contemplated by the IEP must be appropriate in light of the child's circumstances.

"This reflects the focus on the individual child that we have seen throughout the IDEA including in its basic command that a school offer instruction that is in the words of the act specially designed to meet a child's unique needs through an individualized education program.

"Now, our decision in *Rowley* sheds light on what appropriate progress will look like in many cases.

"Although that opinion did not set out an overarching standard, it did say that for children receiving education in the regular classroom, an IEP should generally be 'reasonably calculated to enable the child to achieve passing marks and advance from grade to grade'.

"That guidance is grounded in the text of the IDEA in particular its provisions governing the IEP development process which focus on the pursuit of 'progress in the general education curriculum'.

"*Rowley* did not set out concrete guidance for the case of a child who is not fully integrated in the regular classroom.

"Such a child's IEP need not aim for grade level advancement if that is not a realistic prospect.

"But that child's educational program must be appropriately ambitious in light of his circumstances just as advancement from grade to grade is appropriately ambitious for most children in the regular classroom.

"The goals may differ but every child should have the chance to meet challenging objectives.

"Now, whatever else may be said about this general standard, it is more demanding than the test applied by the Court below.

"It cannot be that the IDEA generally aims for great level advancement for children who are fully intergraded in the regular classroom but tolerates barely more than *de minimis* progress for those who are not.

"Because the adequacy of any IEP turns on the unique circumstances of the child for whom it was crafted, we do not attempt to elaborate on what appropriate progress will look like from case to case.

"A Court should not mistake this absence of a bright line rule for an invitation to override the judgments of educators with their own ideas of educational policy, but at the same time, we differ to school authorities based on their expertise and exercise of judgment.

"The procedure set out in the IDEA ensure that by the time of the dispute about an IEP reaches Court, parents and school representatives will have fully aired their respective views on the degree of progress the IEP should pursue.

"Accordingly, school authorities will have had an opportunity to bring their expertise and judgment to bear on areas of disagreement.

At that point, a reviewing Court may fairly expect those authorities to be able to cogently explain their decisions in a way that shows the IEP is reasonably calculated to enable the child to make progress appropriate in light of his circumstances.

We vacate the judgment below and remand the case for further proceedings.

Our decision is unanimous.

(**Wrightslaw Note: Links to the briefs and the Opinion in the *Endrew* case are located at:**

http://www.scotusblog.com/case-files/cases/endrew-f-v-douglas-county-school-district/

Audio Links to the Oral Argument and this Announcement of the Decision are located at:

https://www.oyez.org/cases/2016/15-827)

This page intentionally left blank for your notes.

Index